100
SIGHTS
of GEORGIA

NODAR ELIZBARASHVILI
BONDO KUPATADZE

Nodar Elizbarashvili, Bondo Kupatadze

100 Sights of Georgia

Edited   **Manana Baliashvili**

Translation
           Guram Abashidze

Design and layout
           Irma Liparteliani
           Elene Varamashvili

Maps   **Zurab Laoshvili**
           Anna Karichashvili

Images   **N. Elizbarashvili, B. Kupatadze, G. Dvalashvili,**
           Agency of Protected Areas and Association "Nekresi"

Copyright © 2011. N. ElizbaraSvili, B. KupataZe
Copyright © 2011. Publishing House "Clio"

ISBN 978-9941-415-33-3

Publishing House "Clio"
Agmashenebeli ave. #181, Tbilisi, 0112, Georgia
Tel.: (+995 32) 34 04 30
E-mail: book@klio.ge
www.klio.ge

Printed in LTD "Favoriti Print", Chubinashvili str. #50, Tbilisi, 0102, Georgia. Tel.: (+995 32) 951-952

GEORGIA'S GEOGRAPHIC SIGHTS

Georgia's landscape variety is outstanding in the world, especially in subtropical and moderate belt. There are more than fifty natural landscapes here, starting from damp subtropical or semiarid light forests to humid and nival landscapes. Such variety has several reasons, the most important of them being as follows: geographic location (on the edge of tropical and moderate belts), high landscape belts (up to 5200 meters above the sea level), and several millennia of land cultivation on this territory.

Georgia is singled out in the world also for its big share of pristine natural environment (territories) which represents 14% of the nation's area. Pristine natural landscape can be found both in protected territories and in high-mountain and mixed relief areas.

Georgia is located in the Caucasus, between the Black and the Caspian seas, surrounded by Russia, Turkey, Armenia and Azerbaijan. Its area is 70 thousand sq. km by which it is on the 25 middle spot in the rankings of the European nations. The formation of the territory of the country counts 600 million years. All kinds of reliefs known in the world are present here. The 2/5 of the territory is covered with forests which is a preeminent ecological asset. There are more than 15 thousand species of plants in Georgia, among them more than 4 thousand types of seminal, 75 filical and 2600 water plants. 6% of flora (or up to 900 species) are endemic and relict. The same kind of variety is typical for the wildlife, among them more than 100 species of mammals and more than 300 birds. By volume, endemism and biovariety of the wildlife Georgia is among the top five European nations which is a vivid proof of its inimitable natural environment.

There are hundreds of natural specimens which make momentous impression on visitors. Among them are dinosaur tracks, enormous and very deep caves, deep and endemic types of canyons, full-flowing rivers having buoyant energy force, lakes and glaciers of different origin, virgin and light forests, semi-deserts and marshes, soils and endemic plants, etc. It is also important that various specimens of nature are concentrated on small spaces that increases their recreational purpose. The bulk of them are located in the protected territories of Georgia.

The protected territories of Georgia have 100-year history. The first sanctuary was established back in 1912, in eastern Georgia, on the southern slope of Caucasus mountains, on the outskirts of the town of Lagodekhi. In the course of a century the space of protected territories has constantly expanded. In Soviet period they were set up to protect wildlife with a status of reserves or conservation areas. In the end of the XX century protected territories of Georgia exist in many categories, national parks enjoying particular popularity. Nowadays the total area of protected territories runs up to 500 thousand hectares that amounts to roughly 7% of the nation's territory. The biggest part of protected territories is covered with forests which, other than having recreational or educational function, carry also huge environmental and regeneration value as well.

GEORGIA'S HISTORICAL SIGHTS

Georgia is the nation of long and complicated history, that is why plethora of historical and cultural monuments are preserved on its territory. These are archeological sights of Stone and Bronze Age, Antique era settlements, Middle Age fortresses, churches and monasteries, bridges and many other memorials.

The geography of the Georgian historical architecture strictly reflects historical developments which took place in Georgia. Construction of bridges and roads is primarily connected with the period of United Georgia (XI-XV centuries AD), that is why these bridges are called among the population *Tamar's bridges*. Fortresses and defense facilities of a large scale basically belong to the early Middle Age period (IV-X centuries AD) when the nation waged important defense wars. In later times these fortresses were renovated. In later Middle Age period primarily feudal towers and relatively smaller castles were erected.

In the course of different development stages of Georgian church architecture different houses of worship were built. Among them the oldest churches belong to a simple hall style. Such churches are constructed up to these days. Starting from V century AD bigger churches – basilicas (two- and three-nave edifices) emerge, and from VII century AD cross-type churches with domes start to be built. From VIII century AD a central-dome style architecture developed in Georgia which reached its apex in X-XI centuries AD cathedrals (Oshki, Bagrat Cathedral, Svetitskhoveli, Alaverdi).

From the outset the Georgian religious architecture primarily experienced influence of Byzantine style (the specimens of this style are two-dome cathedral of Gurjaani, round cathedrals of Gavazi, old Ishkhani, Katskha, Bana which belong to VII-X centuries AD). At the same time original church architecture was under development which has been finally shaped up in XI-XII centuries. Alongside the church architecture Georgian mural painting art made strides, the best specimens of which are dated to X-XIV centuries AD.

Within the space of VIII-X centuries active church development is under way in almost the whole territory of Georgia (however, the southern and western Georgian kingdoms of Tao-Klarjeti and Egrisi-Abkhazeti can be singled out). This is the period when 5 independent political entities take shape on the territory of Georgia and potentate of each one conducts active development. During the period of unified Georgian monarchy (XI-XIII centuries AD) big churches and monasteries were built near administrative centers and strategic venues. In later Middle Ages construction of churches was under way basically in locations and timing where relative peace settled (for example, in Samtskhe – in XIV century AD, in Kakheti – in XVI century AD, in Kartli and Samegrelo – in XVII century AD).

TBILISI

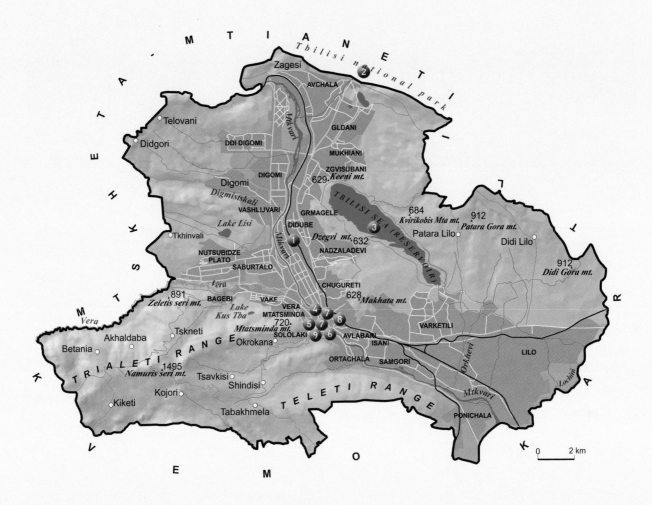

1. Tbilisi – the Capital of Georgia

2. National Park of Tbilisi

3. Tbilisi Sea (Water Pool)

4. Mtatsminda and Mamadaviti (st. Father David)

5. Old Tbilisi

6. Metekhi Cathedral and Narikala

7. Sioni and Kashveti

8. Sameba (Trinity)

9. Synagogue, Mosque and Catholic Church

1 TBILISI — THE CAPITAL OF GEORGIA

Tbilisi is located in the center of the Caucasus, in the plain between mountains, in the gorge of river Mtkvari, in the cavity of the same name, within the 350-900 meters above the sea level, in the latitude of 41°42' and longitude of 44°47', in the close distance from several physical geographic entities (Shida and Kvemo Kartly valley, Iori highland) and historical and geographic provinces (Kvemo Kartli, Trialeti, Shida Kartli and Kakheti).

The area of the city amounts to 500 sq.km (only 40% of the territory is developed), and the population exceeds 1,1 million. The city increased the speed of its development especially from the second half of the XX century. In this period its population grew 2,5-fold and the area – 5-fold. Tbilisi is a multi-ethnic city where people of several religious denominations and dozens of ethnicities live. According to the last census results, after Georgians (84%), the residents of Tbilisi are predominantly Armenians and Russians.

Tbilisi cavity is located between average-height mountain ranges (Trialeti, Saguramo-Ialno) and low mountains (Keeni, Dzedzvi and Makhata). The climate of the city is subtropical dry. The average temperature in January is +0.9°C and in July - +24.4°C. The precipitation volume hovers between 540 mm (southern and eastern parts) and 800 mm (western and northern parts), and evaporation runs up to 900 mm. These weather parameters are based on the natural conditions, the latter being specified by landscape variety. Within the borders of Tbilisi there are 8 types of landscapes (sub-Mediterranean semi-humid, subtropical semi-arid, hydromorphic and sub-hydromorphic, moderately warm humid, etc.) of which one, Tugai grove, is sparse and fragmented.

Within the city boundaries river Mtkvari - the main water artery of the city – is joined by many rivulets and seasonal dry ravines. The length of river Mtkvari here is 35 km. In the environs of the city there are two lakes (lake Lisi and Turtle lake) and one water basin which are the most important recreational facilities.

Tbilisi is the most important economic and transit center of the Caucasus. At about 2/5 of the industrial products manufactured in Georgia are produced here. Abundance of educational institutions, architectural memorials, playhouses, exhibition halls and museums earmarks the city as a cultural and recreational hub in the whole Caucasus.

1. The View of the City from Mount Mtatsminda.
2. New Neighborhood.
3. River Mtkvari Splits the City into Two Parts.

2 NATIONAL PARK OF TBILISI

National Park of Tbilisi is located to the North from Tbilisi, on the slope of Saguramo-lalno range, in the nearest vicinity of the historical and geographic provinces of Shida and Kvemo Kartli, Ertso-Tianeti and Kakheti. Its area is 243 sq. km. It was set up on the basis of a sanctuary of Saguramo which has existed since the mid-XX century.

National Park of Tbilisi belongs to the moderately humid subtropical climate type. Here 4 types of climate are shaped up instigated by forms of relief and exposition. As a result we find here low and average-high mountain landscapes with mixed hornbeam oak, pure oak and beech plants.

Therefore, National Park of Tbilisi is a geographic knot which is an important segment of the emerging unified network of protected territories in the Caucasus.

Among the vegetation we have here up to 700 species including representatives of Colchis flora from the Tertiary period: Colchis holm oak (*Ilex Colchica*), Colchis and Pastukhov ivy (*Hedera colchica, Hedera Pastuchowii*), Caucasus rhododendron, etc.

The wildlife of the National Park of Tbilisi has been under protection of the state for decades. There are several types of big mammals. However, special attention is paid to preservation of a noble Caucasus deer (*Cervus elaphus*).

The protected territory is located near the world-important ancient town of Mtskheta and the capital of Georgia, Tbilisi. On its western border is located Jvari of Mtskheta – highly important Christian monument of the VI century Georgian architecture. There are also many unique archeological and cultural sights part of which are under protection of UNESCO.

3 TBILISI SEA (WATER POOL)

Tbilisi water pool is placed to the east of the city, at the very end of Iori highland. It was created in the beginning of the 50-ies of the XX century on the site of several small ponds. Pool gets its feed primarily from river Iori which is supplied through main Samgori channel.

The area of Tbilisi sea is 11.6 sq. km, and maximal depth is 45 meters. Pool was mainly created for domestic and irrigation purposes due to which the level of water in it seasonally changes. In summer months it has minimal level. The spread of water levels in the pool amounts to 10 meters.

The temperature of Tbilisi sea has rather significant swings (average 18°C). It does not freeze but is characterized by roughness and freezing of beach or thin surface. In July and August water warms up to +26°C and due to it attracts lots of vacationers. In recent years Tbilisi sea has turned into an important recreational facility of the capital of Georgia.

4 MTATSMINDA AND MAMADAVITI (ST. FATHER DAVID)

Mtatsminda, or Mount of st. Father David is located to the west from downtown Tbilisi, at the bifurcation of Trialeti mountain range, 700 meters above the sea level. It is one of the most important natural, historical and cultural sightseeing locations of Georgia. Mtatsminda is covered with artificial pine tree forests and proudly rises over the capital of Georgia.

The spread between downtown Tbilisi and height of Mtatsminda is nearly 400 meters that is why typical effective landscapes and important recreational goal are its natural functions.

From Mtatsminda one can observe the whole view of Tbilisi. To review its panorama there are several lookout terraces. From Mtatsminda one can also see the slope of Kavkasioni mountain range and snowy summit, Saguramo-Ialno mountain range and Iori highland, river Mtkvari and Tbilisi sea. There are different transit options to reach it, the most popular among them being rail track and cable cars.

Nowadays the largest in Georgia theme park and a TV tower are located on Mtatsminda.

Mount of st. Father David rises above the city from the west, its height from the sea level is 727 meters and it is located 330 meters above the sea level from the embankment of river Mtkvari. In the middle of its slope is Church of st. Father David and pantheon of Georgian writers and public figures. The name of the mount and the Church is linked to the life and activity of st.Father David of Gareji – one of the thirteen Assyrian saints. In the middle of the VI century AD he set up here a small site of worship and a cell. Then Mazdeists have expelled st.Father David from the town. In the IX century AD the Church of Virgin Mary of Iveria was built here. That is why the mount of st. Father David has been given a second name – Mtatsminda (means "holy mount"). In the course of time the Church has been damaged. In 1810, under the auspices of Catholicos-Patriarch of Georgia, Anton II, a clergyman of Kashveti, Thoma Grigoriev, with donation financing, erected a church of Transfiguration on Mtatsminda. In 1859 again with the help of public donations, a son of Thoma Grigoriev, Joseph, launched a construction of a new and bigger cathedral of Father David of Gareji which was finished only in 1877. In 1889 mural paintings of the cathedral were completed. The size of the cathedral today is as follows: height (with a cross) - 25, 7 meters, length – 17,2 meters, width – 10,7 meters.

In 1929 Pantheon of Georgian Writers and Public Figures was established in the courtyard of the Church where the most outstanding sons of Georgia have been laid to rest, including: Ilia Chavchavadze, Akaki Tsereteli, Vazha Pshavela, Galaktion Tabidze, the first president of Georgia, Zviad Gamsakhurdia. Famous Russian poet, Alexander Griboedov, and Stalin's mother were also buried in the pantheon.

1. **Mount of Mtatsminda and Funicular Railway**
2. **The Gravesite of the First President of Georgia, Zviad Gamsakhurdia, at Mtatsminda Pantheon**
3. **Church of st. Father David (view from the East)**

5 OLD TBILISI

Old Tbilisi is the historical part of the city, the precincts and neighborhoods of which before 1936 were called Tiflis (in Georgian-Tpilisi). Old Tbilisi compiles the following precincts: Abanotubani-Kharpukhi (thereafter Seidabad), Kala, Isani-Avlabari, Sololaki, Mtatsminda, Vere, Ortachala, Chugureti, Didube, Nadzaladevi. The biggest part of Tbilisi landmarks is concentrated in the Old City, and accordingly it is the major drawcard for the tourists. Since 2007 Old Tbilisi has been a candidate to be included in the UNESCO World Heritage List.

As the story goes, the foundation of the city is linked to the sulphur hot springs on its territory. This story is reflected also in the name of the city ("Tbili" means warm in Georgian). The first settlement in Tbilisi dates back to IV century AD, and in the middle of the V century AD king of Kartli, Vakhtang Gorgasali, started urban development here. His heir Dachi proclaimed Tbilisi the capital of the Kingdom of Kartli. Tbilisi is a natural center of the Caucasus region. Its strategic location has attracted big empires from the times immemorial, and the city often fell under political, economic and cultural influence of foreign nations. In VIII-XII centuries AD Tbilisi was under Muslim domination. It was the seat of Arab emir. In XVI-XVIII centuries it was under the authority of Persia and Ottoman Empire, and in XIX-XX centuries – under the rule of Russia.

In VI-VIII centuries and in XV-XVIII centuries Tbilisi was the capital of Kartli, and in XII-XV centuries – the capital of the Kingdom of Georgia. In 1801-1917 Tbilisi was the center of the region of the Caucasus in the Russian Empire (seat of the Caucasus vicegerant), and in 1918 and 1922-1936 Tbilisi was a principal city of the Trans-Caucasus Federation. In 1918-1921 it was the capital of the Georgian Democratic Republic, and from 1991 – the capital of the independent state of Georgia.

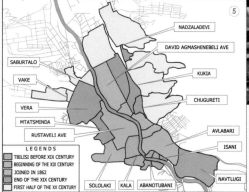

1. Tbilisi in the V century AD (reconstruction)
2. Tbilisi in 1671 (drawing of Jean Chardin)
3. Tbilisi in 1701 (drawing of Turnefore)
4. Tbilisi (beginning of the XX century)
5. Territorial Expansion of Tbilisi in XIX-XX centuries

6 METEKHI CATHEDRAL AND NARIKALA

Metekhi is the oldest settlement of Tbilisi. It is located in Avlabari, on the rocky height of left bank of river Mtkvari. It included Isani stronghold and its environs. It used to be a Royal residence. The very name of *Metekhi* derives from this fact. Metekhi in Old Georgian means 'territory around the palace'. Metekhi was the neighborhood of vendors and artisans. Church of Virgin Mary of Metekhi was located in its center first erected by Vakhnang Gorgasali (V century AD). As the legend goes from old times, at the bottom of Metekhi rock was the venue of martyrdom of the patron saint of Tbilisi, Abo Tbileli (786 AD). Nowadays there is a church named after him.

In 1235 the Mongols destroyed Royal palace standing here and church of the Royal court. In 1278-1289 the Church in modern style was restored by the king of Georgia, Demetre II.

Today's Church is an edifice with a central dome and is a replica of the old church layout. In XVII century AD the *Wali* (potentate) of Kartli, Rostom, circled Metekhi with a fence. In XVII-XVIII centuries cathedral underwent many changes. Persian and Ottoman military were stationed here. During the Russia's rule (from 1801)

the Church was converted into a military barrack. From 1819 ancillary fixtures were attached to Metekhi and until 1938 it used to be a prison. In the 30-ies of the XX century fixtures around the cathedral were demolished and territory was refurbished. The Bolsheviks planned to demolish the cathedral altogether, however they met opposition from the most advanced Georgian intellectuals and reconsidered to carry out this barbarous act. In 1967 in front of the church the monument of the founder of Tbilisi, Vakhtang Gorgasali, was installed (sculptor – E. Amashukeli). From 1988 Metekhi church started service operation.

Narikala is a historical citadel and main fortress of Tbilisi. In Georgian sources it is called 'Mother Fortress'. The term 'Narikala' is a Persian word and was used to call the fortress in XVII century. Narikala has the traces of numerous reconstructions conducted in IV-XVIII centuries. The last reconstruction at Narikala was conducted in 2000. The Church of St. Nicholas and a fence were restored, the latter got a complete form. From Narikala fortress one may enjoy the most beautiful views of Old and New Tbilisi.

1. Metekhi and Narikala (view from North-East)
2. Metekhi Cathedral and Meidan (Tatar Square) (beginning of XX century)
3. Narikala and Kalaubani (beginning of XX century)

7 SIONI AND KASHVETI

Cathedral of St. Virgin Mary (Sioni) was built on the edge of VI-VII centuries AD. This is the main Christian cathedral of Tbilisi. Due to pillage of invaders, the cathedral went through numerous changes. In 1226 the Shah of Khorezm, Jalal-ed-Din, conquered Tbilisi. On his order the dome of Sioni was removed and his throne placed instead. Sitting on this throne he viewed those Georgians who refused to abuse the icons of Our Savior and Virgin Mary which were carried from the church and placed on the Metekhi bridge. That day 100 000 Christians were beheaded. In 1522 Sioni cathedral was ravaged by Shah of Iran, Ismail.

In 1675 Bishop Elise Saginashvili on the order of king Rostom attached a small chapel to the building of Sioni from the southern side, and placed a new dome on the cathedral. In 1710 Vakhtang VI made an outer facing of the Cathedral with the tuff. During this restoration ornaments and carvings were applied which adorn the Cathedral today.

During the Russian rule Sioni again sustained changes. In the 50-ies of the XIX century Grigori Gagarin made new mural paintings. In 1867 Sioni cathedral again renewed its existence. The last refurbishment works were conducted in Sioni in 1983. The Church of Michael the Archangel was set up in the southern chapel, and in the northern chapel – the Church of Vakhtang Gorgasali. New cross was installed on the dome.

The Sioni cathedral has two belfries. The bell tower deep in the court to the north of the cathedral dates back to 1725. To the west of the cathedral, on the other side of the street three-level bell tower with a spire was built in 1812 and represents the first specimen of Russian classicism.

The Kashveti church was first erected as a small chapel by the Holy Saint, Father David of Gareji. In 1753 due to damage to the cathedral, commander of the special military district (*sadrosho*) of Shida Kartly, Givi Amilakhvari, built it with brick. The legend on this

construction has been preserved on the left wall from the gates of a lower cathedral. Construction of today's Kashveti cathedral started on November 12, 1904. The architects were L-P. Billiefeld, E. L. Andreoletti, brothers Agladze with the chief financier – David Sarajishvili.

The contemporary Kashveti was designed according to the layout of the church of Samtavisi. Its architectural feature is non-traditional location of iconostasis. Iconostasis is not placed between front columns but behind them in order to grant more space to clerics rather than worshippers. The construction used Algeti stone, Dzegami white stone, Italian marble. Cathedral has a plain ornament. Ornaments are picked from various churches of Georgia and are harmoniously dovetailed. The altar of the Cathedral is painted by a notable Georgian painter, Lado Gudiashvili.

1. Sioni (view from the East)
2. Donator Inscription of Vakhtang VI (Western façade of Sioni, 1710)
3. Kashveti (view from South-West)

8 SAMEBA (TRINITY)

Sameba cathedral was built on the edge of millenium under the auspices of Catholikos-Patriarch of All Georgia, Ilia II, and simbolically expresses liberation of Georgia on the verge of millenium and revival of the Christian faith. Tender on the design of the Cathedral was held in 1988. Construction started in 1995 according to the design of architect Archil Mindiashvili, and was finished in 2004.

The Sameba cathedral consists of 5 underground and 4 aboveground churches. Those are churches of Archangel, John the Baptist, St. Nino, St. George, St. Nicholas, 12 Prophets and All Saints.

Sameba cathedral is the highest and largest church in Georgia. Its space exceeds 5 thousand sq. meters. It is equipped with the state-of-the-art communication, power, heating and conditioning systems. The height until the bottom of a cross is 86 meters, the height of a cross is 7,5 meters. Underground part of the Cathedral consists of two levels and is 14 meters deep from earth surface. The architecture of the Cathedral is a mixture of old Georgian religious architectural styles of cross and central dome. Holy Sameba Cathedral is triptych implanted within the cross with a dome buttressed by eight pillars.

It is possible to enter the Cathedral from three sides – portals are arranged in three (western, southern and

northern) arms. Among them the main gateway is in the western arm which has a wide gallery attached from the outside.

Bell tower of Sameba cathedral is a three-level building. Its length is 20 meters, width – 8 meters, height – 29.5 meters.

1. Holy Sameba Cathedral (general view)
2. Holy Sameba Cathedral

9 SYNAGOGUE, MOSQUE AND CATHOLIC CHURCH

Jews are the ancient residents of Georgia. Back in VI century BC part of the persecuted Jewish people from Jerusalem arrived and settled in Mtskheta. Jews had their own neighborhoods in almost all big cities of Georgia and they were primarily engaged in trade. Closely settled Jews constructed their house of worship – a synagogue. There are many synagogues on the territory of Georgia, including synagogue in Oni, province of Racha, known for its beauty and original architectural forms. There are several synagogues in Tbilisi. Active big synagogue is located on Leselidze street. It was built in 1910. There is also a small synagogue nearby. The third so called *Dome Synagogue* is on Anton Katalikos street. It is not operating now and there has been set up David Baazov Historical and Ethnographic Museum of Georgian Jews.

Nearly 4 centuries (735-1122) Tbilisi was under Islamic influence. Historical sources tell us that a mosque in Tbilisi has existed from VIII century AD. Thereafter the influence of Islamic culture on the lifestyle and architecture of the city was big. Located in downtown, not far from Botanical garden, the mosque was first built by the king of Kartli, Rostom (1633-1658). In XIX century a minaret of the mosque underwent a reconstruction by an Italian architect Giovanni Scudieri. There was another mosque on the left bank of river Mtkvari, in Rike, which was built in 1522 on the order of Shah of Iran, Ismail. This Shiite mosque was demolished by the communists under the pretext of reconstructing Metekhi bridge. After that both denominations of Islam (Shiites and Sunnis) pray in the Sunni mosque in Abanotubani neighborhood.

The first Catholic church in Tbilisi was built by Dominican monks back in 1243. During the reign of Giorgi V Brilliant (1318-1346), on the order of the Roman Pope, a diocese was set up in Tbilisi and Catholic Church of Annunciation was built, presumably, at the same venue where it is today (at the gateway of historical Tbilisi, near the gates of Kojori. Today - 4 Abesadze st.). In 1795 Shah of Iran, Agha Mahmad Khan, during his invasion of Tbilisi demolished along with others also Catholic church. In 1804 under initiative of a vicegerent Pavel Tsitsianov a plan of a pseudo-Gothic style new church was designed, construction of which was finished in 1806 (fence was finished in 1825). The Church of Holy Virgin Mary functioned up to 20-ies of the XX century until it was shut down by the Bolsheviks. In 1998-1999 under the auspices of Bishop G. Pezotti the Church was renovated and became operational.

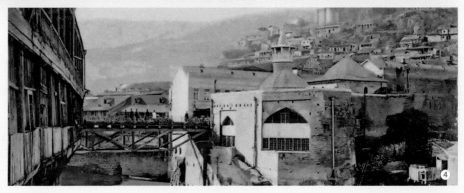

1. Tbilisi's Great Synagogue
2. Abanotubani and Tbilisi Mosque
3. Catholic Church in Tbilisi
4. Shiite Mosque in Rike
   (photo of XIX century)

IMERETI

10. **Dinosaur's Tracks – Imereti Cave Compound**

11. **Ajameti Conservation Area**

12. **Colchis Lowland**

13. **River Rioni and City of Kutaisi**

14. **Tskhaltubo**

15. **Gelati**

16. **Bagrat Cathedral**

17. **Royal Residences – Geguti Palace and Golden Chardakhi**

18. **Katskhi and Motsameta**

19. **Ubisa**

20. **Vani**

10 DINOSAUR'S TRACKS — IMERETI CAVE COMPOUND

In 1933 up to 200 unique tracks of a predator and herbivorous dinosaurs were discovered in Western Georgia, 260 km from Tbilisi, on the marl limestone. The venue is located on the 500 m above the sea level, in the humid subtropical climate zone, on the windy slopes of the western exposition (Black Sea winds). The annual precipitation here runs up to 2000 mm.

Near dinosaur tracks there are several karst caves. Among them the joint length of the biggest of them amounts to several hundreds of meters and the height is 10 meters. Aiming at preservation of dinosaur tracks and caves, in 1935 a reserve was set up based on which a sanctuary was developed. The site preserves other than speleological, also geological, paleontological, zoological and botanical attractions. The biggest part of the territory is covered by Colchis forests in the lower part of which dominate evergreen and deciduous species of plants and bushes.

There are more than seventy species of plants at the sanctuary with the area of 3,5 sq. m. Three types of highest plants are endemic for the Caucasus and one – for Georgia. More than half of tree-plants are relicts of Tertiary period which is a rare case for the territories located in the likely latitudes. From the relicts the following species should be singled out: Caucasus hornbeam (*Carpinus caucasica*), Georgian oak (*Quercus iberica*), Eastern beech (*Fagus orientalis*), chestnut tree (*Castanea sativa*), Imereti buckthorn (*Rhamnus imeretina*), ordinary alder-tree (*Alnus barbata*), Colchis Bladdernut (*Staphylea pinnata*), mistletoe (*Buxus colchica*), et al. Mistletoe in the form of coppice creates taiga forest, the age of several of which attains a century. There are more than 50 wildlife species of which the population of birds is noted for its variety.

In the vicinity of the sanctuary there are many historical and archeological monuments. Among them should be mentioned ancient settlement of Vani, early Middle Age church of Ubisi, church Motsameta, Gelati Monastery Complex under protection of UNESCO, and Bagrat Cathedral.

AJAMETI CONSERVATION AREA

Ajameti Conservation Area is located in Western Georgia, at the eastern end of Colchis lowland, 265 km from Tbilisi. It was founded on the site of a reserve of the same name which had functioned since 1946.

The territory of conservation area is 5 sq. km and is mostly covered by polidominant ancient Colchis forests. From plant species widely represented are oak, hornbeam, orchid, elm, winghut, walnut tree, et al. In the taiga forest we see evergreen rhododendron, Pastukhov ivy, medlar, rosehip, et al. Such relict species are protected here as well as Imereti oak (*Quercus imeretina*), zelkova (*Zelciva carpinifolia*). The age of some tree species attains several centuries.

The wildlife of Ajameti conservation area is relatively poor. However, there are some species which have been included in the Red Book of Georgia: small bat noctule, Caucasus squirrel, dormouse, forest dormouse, and Caucasus otter.

On the environs of Ajameti conservation area there are numerous monuments of big importance. Among them are settlement Vartsikhe (was built on the ruins of Antique township Rodopolis), Geguti (XI century ruins of Hunters' Palace), the city of Kutaisi, et al.

Colchis combining plain lowland is located in Western Georgia, up to 200 meters above the sea level. It has a form of a triangle with its bottom attached to the sea coast. It is a former hollow of the sea which was filled with river rocks. The western part of the lowland is sinking which is a cause of frequent flooding and marshing effect.

Colchis lowland has a small slant, therefore the flow of rivers on it is weak. They create meanders which facilitate formation of frame lakes. In the vicinity of Black sea there are marshes which are located on the routes of migrant birds.

Colchis lowland is a hub where moist (western) and dry (eastern) blowing winds mix. Eastern winds facili-

tate evaporation of excessive moist and good harvest. However, due to them, in summertime hot and stifling weather takes shape followed sometimes by drought and destruction of harvest.

Colchis lowland from the times immemorial was a venue of human settlement and husbandry. Ancient Greek colonies were present here, and the legend on Argonauts and Golden Fleece is also linked to Colchis. Nowadays the lowland is heavily settled (150-200 persons per sq. m) and is almost fully occupied. Natural environment here has been preserved only in the sanctuary and on the highly damp territories.

13 RIVER RIONI AND THE CITY OF KUTAISI

River Rioni flows in Western Georgia, across the territory of several historical and geographic provinces – Racha, Imereti, Guria and Samegrelo. It is noted by its water stream (13,22 km³) and catchment area (13,4 km²). The catchment area comprises 41% of the territory of Western Georgia.

Deep down in history river Rioni was called *Phasis*. This name is tied to Colchis pheasant having its natural habitat in its groves. Europeans have become familiar with it through Argonauts. On the path of its flow the river creates islands and various forms of relief (canyon-like gorges, mountain gates, groves, terraces, meanders). Its ravine is noted with various landscapes linked with relief and climate conditions. In the catchment area of river Rioni there are more than 10 types of landscapes developed in the moist subtropical, moderately warm humid and moderately cold weather conditions. It is possible to visit them within 2-3 hour trip and get unforgettable impressions.

In the middle of the flow of river Rioni is located the second largest city of Georgia, Kutaisi. It is settled on the both banks of the river, at 150-300 meters above the sea level. It has moist subtropical climate. In mid-January average temperature is +5.2°C, in July - +23.2°C, the volume of precipitation (1380 mm) is nearly 1,5 times more than evaporation.

Archeological excavations prove that in the VI century BC there was a township there. For many centuries it played the role of important political, administrative, cultural and educational center of Georgia. Within the boundaries of the city of Kutaisi there are numerous important natural, historical and cultural sights. Not far from the city are located Sataplia sanctuary territories, Ajameti conservation area, the Pole of Katskhi, Tsutskhvati Cave, Khvamli mountain range and other natural sightseeing locations.

1. Kutaisi (view from Ukimerion Mount)
2. Mew restored centre of Kutaisi
3. R. Rioni da white bridge

RESORT TSKHALTUBO AND TSKHALTUBO CAVE

Tskhaltubo is a spa well-known in the world which is located in Western Georgia, on 100-120 meters above the sea level. It is operated during the whole year. The spa is in 250 kilometers from Tbilisi and in 7 km from Kutaisi.

The natural environment of the spa is noted with impressive landscapes. Within its boundaries there are forest and kastral landscapes of Colchis valley, low and medium-size mountains. The climate is moist subtropical. Average temperature in January is +5,2°C, and in July - +23°C. Average annual precipitation is 1700-1800 mm which is increased in the surrounding mountains. Such kind of moisture duly supplies underground thermal waters a day-and-night debit of which attains 20 million litres.

Curative qualities of Tskhaltubo thermal waters have been known for centuries, however as a spa it started operation from 1926. Mineralization of waters here is 0,7-0,8 mg/l and temperature is +33+35°C. They are used for baths, inhalations and sprays. Thermal waters are very effective treatment for rheumatism, bones, nerves, cardio-vascular system, skin and gynecological diseases.

Not far from the spa is Tskhaltubo cave which by its scope is one of the most remarkable in Europe.

15 GELATI

Gelati monastery complex is located in 11 km to the north-east from the city of Kutaisi, in the gorge of river Tskaltsitela. The monastery was founded by the king of Georgia, David IV Agmashenebeli (1089-1125). The territory of the monastery is restricted by a fence and consists of 5 constructions. These edifices are the main cathedral of the Assumption of Virgin Mary (1106, sizes of the Cathedral: 35m x 36m x 34m), church of St. George to the east of the main cathedral (XII century AD), two-level church of St. Nicholas (XII-XIV centuries), bell tower with stone arch built over spring to the north-west from the main cathedral, and a building of Gelati Academy.

The main cathedral is embellished with limestone and is rich with mural paintings. In the arch of the altar the mosaic of Gelati is preserved (the Virgin Mary with adolescent, Archangels Michael and Gabriel), in the western entrance there is a XII century fresco with the image of a church assembly; in the southern eukterion there are two portraits of the king of Georgia, David VI Narin (1246-1293) (in royal garments and casual national costume – *chokha*); on the northern wall there are images of the members of Imereti royal family (XVI century), next is the portrait of David IV Agmashenebeli (1089-1125) restored in XVI century.

To the south of the fence of Gelati monastery, in the main entrance, there is a tombstone of David Ag-mashenebeli (the tomb itself presumably is in the church). According to historical sources, Gelati was the burial site of the united Georgia kings, and all kings of XII-XIII centuries (David IV, Demetre I, Giorgi III, Tamar, Giorgi IV) and kings of Imereti of XVI-XIX centuries (Bagrat III, Giorgi II,

Giorgi III, Aleksandre V, Solomon I, the last Georgian king Solomon II) are laid to rest in Gelati.

Gelati was a royal monastery in XII-XV centuries and reported directly to the king and the first minister (*Mtsignobartukhutsesi*). Rector of Gelati Academy, or Chief Confessor at the royal court, was considered to be a high profile figure, arguably tantamount to Catholicos. The senior monkhood of the monastery were members of the Royal Council.

In the 20-ies of the XVI century Bishop cathedra was set up in Gelati, and at the end of XVI century the seat of the Catholicos-Patriarch of Western Georgia was removed from Bichvinta to a more secure venue in Gelati. In various times the richest Georgian manuscripts and national treasure (Khakhuli Icon of the Virgin Mary) were kept in Gelati. In 1923 the Bolsheviks closed the monastery. Its renovation occurred in 1990.

Gelati Academy – the most important education center in the medieval Georgia - is part of the Gelati monastery complex. People of those times compared Academy with Jerusalem and Athens, since education process here embodied traditions of Antique and Christian sciences. Along with learning process, the Academy was noted for translation and scientific research activity and creation of original works.

1. **Fresco of XVI century in Gelati: the family of the Imereti king Bagrat III, Giorgi the Chief Chancellor (Mtsignobartukhutsesi) and David Agmashenebeli (the northern wall of the Church of St. George)**
2. **Dome**
3. **Churches of St. George and St. Nicholas at Gelati**

BAGRAT CATHEDRAL

Cathedral of the Assumption of the Virgin Mary constructed by the king of the Abkhaz and the Georgians, Bagrat III (978-1014), on the Ukimerion Mount is the main landmark of Kutaisi. Here the Georgian monarchs were ordained as kings, and the enthronization was conducted by Kutaisi Bishop. As per the legend on the northern wall of the cathedral, construction of the cathedral was finished in 1003. Bagrat cathedral, like Svetitskhoveli, Oshki, Alaverdi holds a special place in the history of Georgian architecture. It is a brilliant example of the Georgian church style of X-XI centuries. There are presumptions that Georgian kings of XI century (Giorgi I, Bagrat IV) were laid to rest there.

In the first half of the XI century rich ornamented gates were attached to the cathedral from south and west which were preserved until 30-ies of the XIX century. Bagrat cathedral is rich with adornment and ornaments, especially with decorations of tops of windows and gates. Bases and column tops are decorated with bas-relief images. Floor was decorated with mosaic.

Sadly enouph, nowadays the cathedral is very damaged. According to the report of Vakhushti Bagrationi in 1692, the Ottomans have toppled the dome of the cathedral. In the course of time its destruction continued. Today the Foundation for the Revival of Bagrat Cathedral has been set up with the aim of reconsting the cathedral using state-of-the-art technologies. Since 1994 Bagrat cathedral has been listed in the UNESCO World Cultural Heritage list. In 1995 church service was renewed in the cathedral. In 2009 the government of Georgia launched works for full restoration of the Cathedral.

1. Bagrat Cathedral (general view from west)
2. Remains of fence
3. Bagrat Cathedral at present

ROYAL RESIDENCES —
GEGUTI PALACE AND GOLDEN CHARDAKHI

The only remaining palace and residence of Georgian royals, today however in ruins, is located in 7 km to the south from Kutaisi, on the bank of river Rioni. Its area is 2 000 sq.m. In VIII-X centuries it was a country retreat– a hunting house - for the Abkhaz kings. From XI century it became a residence of the Georgian kings. According to *Kartlis Tskhovreba,* in XII century a four-level royal palace hall was built. The main part of the palace had a 14-meter dome above it. It was a 4-nave hall with living quarters on both sides (sleeping room, cash-room, treasury, bathroom). On the west part of the palace is a church (XIII-XIV centuries).

Golden *Chardakhi* on the right bank of river Rioni, in downtown Kutaisi, between today's Rustaveli and White bridges was the residence of Imereti kings. First reports on the royal residence belong to European travellers (Italian Ambrozio Contarini in XV century and Russian ambassadors Tolochanov and

Ievlev in XVII century). The residence had several constructions: Court church of St. George, Big House, Small House and Dinner Chamber. In the center of a courtyard under plane trees of which one has remained up to nowadays was a table on four pillars for feasts. In the wall of a fence was arranged a belfry and a lookout point for guards of a king's cash-room and Royal Palace.

In XVII century Royal residence was damaged many times. For XIX century of all constructions of the residence only Small House, Court church and belfry have survived.

Today the only surviving construction of the royal residence is so called Small House. The first level was designed to protect from flooding and is equipped with arches from all sides. The walls of the Big hall on the second level are decorated with combat scene paintings. The constriction was remade in the XIX century and received today's image in the 1960-ies.

1. Geguti Palace (general view)
2. Geguti Palace. Big hall
3. Golde Chardakhi
4. R. Rioni and Golde Chardakhi

18 KATSKHI AND MOTSAMETA

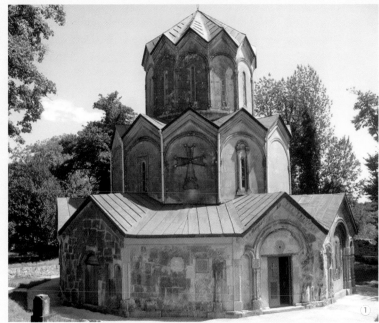

The Katskhi Church of Saviour is located in the hamlet of Katskhi, in the gorge of river Katskhura, in Chiatura region. Cathedral was built at the beginning of XI century. Its main parts were constructed in 1010 -1014 by the feudal family of Bagvashi (on the main entrance of the edifice one can see segments of the Bagvashi family coat of arms: lion and elderly angel). Katskhi was their family church and venue for burial. In Katskhi was laid to rest one of the most powerful and noted feudals, Liparit IV Bagvashi (died in 1064). After downfall of the family of Bagvashi and their extradition from Georgia Katskhi cathedral has been ravaged. In XVI century neglected and damaged cathedral was resuscitated by its new holder Abulasar Amirejibi. In XVII-XVIII centuries Katskhi belonged to the family of Abashidze, and from 50-ies of the XVIII century it was transferred to the management of Royal administration.

Katskhi is surrounded by five-angle fence. It has old bell tower with the function of a gate. Katskhi cathedral is one of the outstanding and original monuments of the Georgian religious architecture. There is no other architectural feat with the same form. Construction consists of three staggering parts: outer space, building of a church and a neck of a dome. It is a six-apse cathedral. The construction used to be decorated with rich ornaments. However, as a result of a restoration conducted by the Exarchate of the Russian church in 1854, ornaments were removed and frescos were painted. On the tops of all entrances to the church there are bas-reliefs (primarily with images of lion). All bas-reliefs of the cathedral have inscriptions in *Asomtavruli*. Most of the legends are in tittles.

Motsameta church is located within 6 km distance from Kutaisi to the East, in the gorge of river Tskaltsitela. The history of its foundation is linked to the names of the nobles of Argveti, David and Konstantine Mkheidze. They were detained by *Murvan Kru* who invaded Georgia in 736-738 and punished them to death for fidelity to Christianity. The church has beatified martyred heroes as saints. Their Holy Remains at first were laid to rest at the destroyed Annunciation church. In XI century Bagrat III rebuilt destroyed church and reburied martyrs to this church. In 1844-65 under the auspices of the Bishop of Imereti, David Tsereteli, Motsameta was refurbished and expanded. Dome was mounted on the cathedral, stone flooring made and iconostasis changed. In 1923 the Bolsheviks closed the church and exhumed Holy Remains from the tomb and threw them into the water. The local residents managed to save Holy Remains. They were handed over to the museum of Kutaisi. Motsameta has restarted its function in 1954. The bodies of David and Konstantine were carried from the museum and reburied in the church. The holiday of Motsameta is celebrated on October 15.

1. Church of Katskhi
2. Monastery of Motsameta (general view)

19 UBISA

Within the distance of 160 km to the West from Tbilisi, to the left from the backbone expressway, in Kharagauli region, is located Ubisi Monastery Complex. It consists of the church of St. George (was founded in IX century by the disciples of Grigol Khandzteli, Christephore and Theodore), 4-level tower with column (the *Asomtavruli* legend of the church tells that this tower was built by the first minister of the Kingdom of Georgia, Svimon Chkondideli, Chief Chancellor, in 1141), residue of the fence and lean-to of XVI century.

Cathedral and tower are constructed with pumice stone, they are plainly ornamented and walls have some construction inscriptions. The main attractions of Ubisi are XVI century mural paintings performed by Damiane. Here are brilliant compositions of all Holy celebrations: Annunciation, Palm Sunday, Crucifixion, Resurrection, Epiphany, etc. Among the murals Fresco of St. George of Ubisi and Last Supper can be singled out. These paintings represent mixture of Georgian and Byzantine style of painting.

1. Monastery of Ubisi (general view)
2. Ubisi Alter (artist Damiane)
3. Donator Inscription of Svimon Mtsignobartukhutsesi (1141)
4. Monastery of Ubisi. Front entrance

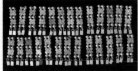

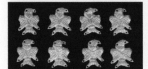

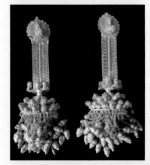

20 VANI

This is the most important town of Antique era Colchis. The town was composed of many settlements available around. In the history of Antique Vani two periods can be sorted out: VI-IV centuries and III-I centuries BC. On the first stage Vani was the center of administrative entity of the Colchis Kingdom (Skeptukhia) and residence of governing elite. Wooden cult and domestic fixtures, diverse ceramics (black-polished, black and red figurines, clay and metal utensils) and rich burial sites (diadems, bracelets, necklaces, earrings, pendants, heraldic images and cups) which prove close trade, economic and cultural ties with the Greek world, belong to this epoch.

In the second stage Vani became a big temple center. Archeological excavations discovered fence walls, round temple, buttress construction, seven-step alter, figurines for cult and ritual worship, local and Greek ceramic artefacts. In I century BC the Antique town ceased to exist.

1. Vani Archeological Museum
2. Alter of Heathen Temple
3. Vani Excavations and Discovered Digging Material

KAKHETI

21. **Vashlovani Reserve Territories**
22. **Tusheti Reserve Territories**
23. **Batsara-Babaneuri Reserve Territories**
24. **Lagodekhi Reserve Territories**
25. **Signaghi**
26. **Bodbe**
27. **Telavi and Batonis Tsikhe (Master's Fortress)**
28. **Tsinandali**
29. **Ikalto and Shuamta**
30. **Alaverdi**
31. **Gremi and Nekresi**
32. **Gurjaani Kvelatsminda and Kvetara**
33. **David Gareji Monastery Complex**

21 VASHLOVANI RESERVE TERRITORIES

Vashlovani Reserve Territories are located in south-eastern part of Georgia, 160 km from Tbilisi, at the end of Upland Iori, between rivers Iori and Alazani. It encompasses a sanctuary, national park and three natural memorials with total area of 250 sq. km.

The climate of reserve territory is moderately moist subtropical where volume of precipitation attains 400 mm. Even slight change of the exposition here is the cause of changes in the moisture of soil and ultimately a landscape. Nowadays within its frame are represented semi-desert and badlands, steppes and shibliak, arid thin forests and pine tree landscapes.

Flora of Vashlovani reserve territories is of savannah type on the backdrop of which steppes and frigana bushes are represented with grass and needle grass. Here we have very rare pistachio tree (Pistacea mutica), Tugai forests of arid regions with inclusions of oak (Qurcus pedunculata), asp (Populus nigra, Populus canescens), ash-tree (Fraxinus excelsior), wild granate (Punica granatum) and walnut (Juglans regia).

There are several hundred species of plants in Vashlovani, among them should be mentioned 7 species of orchids, Georgian iris (Iris iberica), tulip of Eichler (Tulipa eichler), wild vane (Vitis sylvestris), et al. The fauna of reserve territories is also diversified, especially there are plenty of birds. Here also 'rest' a lot of migrant birds. From birds of prey there are Eastern Imperial eagles (Aquila heliaca), griffon, eagle (Gyps fulvus), hen-harrier (Circus aeroginosusu) and buzzard (Buteo buteo). There are lots of Colchis pheasants (Phasianus colchicus) in the groves. In the badlands of Vashlovani thousands of swallows make their nests and colonies. Such places are called City of Swallows.

Natural conditions create favorable environment for the reptiles. It is possible to see here Mediterranean turtle, Asian boa constrictor, four-strip swimmer, regular grass snake, blunt-nosed viper and many other species. Number of insect species attains 700, among them 1/7 are butterflies.

There are many types of animals in the reserve territories. Among them are bears (Ursus arctos) rare for the arid places. At the end of 2003 front-Asian snow leopard (Pantera pardus ciscaucasica) was found in Vashlovani which later became a symbol of Vashlovani.

Recently gazelle (Gazella subgutturosa subgutturosa) was brought from neighboring countries which in near past was represented in big numbers on the adjacent territories.

Sightseeing of the unique environmental variety of Vashlovani reserve territories is possible for any visitor. Tourist infrastructure is well developed here.

22 TUSHETI PROTECTED TERRITORIES

Tusheti protected territories are located in Northern Georgia, 250 km from Tbilisi, in the extreme north-eastern part of the nation, on the borderline with the Russian Federation (Dagestan and Chechnia). It consists of three categories of preserved territory – a state sanctuary, a National park and a protected landscape. Preserved territories cover Tusheti fully which is one of the notable and one-of-a-kind historical and geographic province of Georgia. Its total area exceeds 1220 sq.m (which is 1,7% of the territory of Georgia and 0,3% of that of the Caucasus).

Diversity of Tusheti natural environment, vertical staggering levels and well-formed natural barriers determine variety of wildlife, its unique and endemic character. Both in terms of quantity and quality of species Tusheti is distinguished in the whole Caucasus. Here are represented 1/5 share of endemics in the whole region.

From endemic species widely spread in Tusheti, there are: Tusheti aconite, barberries, bluebell (Campanula), Georgian nuts, starling (Pancratium), Tusheti rosehip (Rosa tuschetica), black or Radde birch (Betula raddena), arum (Fritillaria caucasica), primrose (Primula juliae), et al.

In Tusheti there are more than 200 species of fauna most of which are birds. There are many endemics as well, namely, East Caucasus aurochs, chamois and saiga, Caucasian snowcock and Caucasian black crouse. There is a lot of roebuck and wild boar in the forest, as well as wolf and brown bear can be found sometimes.

Tusheti is distinguished with specifics and unique character of historical and architectural monuments, folk handicrafts, traditions and ethnic culture, agriculture (especially livestock).

23 BATSARA—BABANEURI PRESERVED TERRITORIES

Batsara-Babaneuri Preserved Territories are located in Eastern Georgia, 150-170 km from Tbilisi, on the southern slopes of Kakheti Kavkasioni range of mountains. They consist of several parts being one entity from management point. Its total area is more than 90 sq. km.

The first segment of preserved territories encompasses the middle body of river Batsara gorge. Yew forest (Taxus baccata), a relict of Tertiary period, has been preserved here with the area (240 ha) outstanding in the world. The age of plant trees runs several hundred years, and height of leafage exceeds 40 meters. Pastukhov's ivy (Hedera pastuchowii) and greenberries (Snilax excelsa) are widely spread in the forest that creates unforgettable impression.

The Babaneuri segment is located in the south-east part of the preserved territories and encompasses lowland and hillock mountain territories. Here is preserved the relict of the Tertiary period and Caucasian endemic – the forest of zelkova (Zelqova caprinifolia) with the area of 750 ha.

The segment of Ilto is located in the western part of the preserved territories and encompasses the gorge of the same name of the river where there are unchanged beeches (Fagus orientalis) preserved. In the underbush cherry laurel is lavish. And virgin beeches create unforgettable impression on the visitors.

The fauna of the preserved territory is multifarious where some tens of mammal species and fifty species of birds have their habitat, with trout in the rivers.

Near the preserved territories there are archeological monuments of the Bronze Age – the Medieval cathedral Alaverdi, Ikalto Academy, Shuamta monastery complex, Gremi Temple-city and many other historical and architectural attraction.

24 LAGODEKHI PRESERVED TERRITORIES

Lagodekhi preserved territories are located in the north-eastern part of Georgia, on the border with Dagestan and Azerbaijan, within the Kavkasioni mountain range in Kakheti, on the 400-3500 meters above the sea level. Overall area of the territory is 244 sq.m. It consists of two parts – a sanctuary and conservation area. Lagodekhi preserved territories are the oldest in the Caucasus and its environment received a sanctuary status at the beginning of the last century. Sanctuary which was founded in 1912 was linked to the great number of endemic species. There are more than 100 species of plants which are endemic for the Caucasus and Georgia and identify exceptional character of the preserved territory.

The relief of the preserved territory is 'guttered' with gorges of rivers and many waterfalls. Here is also rather deepwater Black Rock lake which in the Alpine zone creates inimitable landscape.

Relatively long history of Lagodekhi preserved territories has been vividly reflected on the environment. Here is well represented vertical zone of natural conditions, pristine environment of nature, landscape and biovariety.

The largest area in the preserved territories is occupied by beech forest, second come alder groves, hornbeam groves and oak groves. In the sub-Alpine zone oak groves, birch wood and rhododendron bushes are extended.

The fauna of the preserved territories is rich and diverse where the bulk of species are birds (150 species) and mammals (53 species). Such animals as lynx (Lynx lynx), wolf (Canis lupus), brown bear (Ursus arctos), chamois (Rupicapra rupicapra), Caucasian aurochs (Capra cylindricornis), deer (Cervus elaphus), roebuck (Capreolus capreolus), boar (Sus scofa), lammergeyer (Gypaetos barbatus), mountain eagle (Aquila heliaca), falcon (Falco peregrinis), mountain (Aquila chrysaetus fulva) and valley (Aquila nipalensis) eagle, Eastern Imperial Eagle (Aquila heliaca), Caucasian heath cock (Tetrao mlokosiewiczi) and Caucasian mountain turkey (Teatraogalus caucasicus) have established here their habitat.

In the vicinity of preserved territories there are numerous important historical and archeological monuments. Among them are pre-Christian settlements and graves, early Christian and Middle Age churches and fortresses.

25 SIGNAGHI

The town of Signaghi is located in Eastern Georgia, at the end of the Tsivgombori mountain range, on its south-eastern slopes, 110 km from Tbilisi, 800 meters above the sea level. It is overlooking the Alazani valley and the height of Signaghi over it is more than 400 meters. Alazani ravine and the upright standing mountains at the backdrop create unforgettable view and attract numerous tourists. Signaghi is one of the oldest towns in Georgia which was given its status in 1801. In spite of small number of residents (2150) it still plays the role of important economic and cultural center of Kakheti.

The climate is moderately damp, however in summertime it has annual precipitation share of 7,5% thanks to which there is lack of moisture. The average temperature in January is nary more than 0°C, and in July — $+23^{\circ}$C. Natural flora is almost rearranged. Nowadays, along with the cultural plants, there are landscapes typical for dry gorges and semi-deserts, steppes, forest steppes (arid forests) and leafy forest landscapes. Such variety is an important resource for educational tourism.

Signaghi and its environs are peppered with ancient churches and monasteries, historical monuments and museums. They are visited every year by tens of thousands of worshippers and holiday-makers.

The name Signaghi is of Turkish origin and means 'shelter'. It has been a fortress since XIII-XIV centuries. The transformation of Signaghi into a town is related to the king of Kartli-Kakheti, Erekle II. He founded the Royal town in 1762 and settled there 100 families of merchants and artisans and surrounded the town with the big fence made of a mixture of cobblestone and brick. The fence of Signaghi is one of the biggest in Georgia. Its length is up to 4 km and it encircles almost 40 ha. The fence has two levels. The lower, blind one has the width of 1,5 meters and the upper level – 70-80 sm. The width difference of these layers creates a path for conducting combat. There are 23 built-in towers on the fence (equipped with 2-3 levels, with rifle emplacements, fireplace and combat platforms). Each tower bears the name of an adjacent village. There are five gates in the fence, among them central, minegate, is directly connected with the fortress. Church of St. Stepane Khirseli was built within the fortress fence of Signaghi.

In 2005-2008 with support of the Ministry of Culture and the President of Georgia Signaghi was rehabilitated. Infrastructure was changed, streets were refurbished, and the buildings were given their original appearance.

1. Signaghi (general view from Didtsveri mountain)
2. Signaghi Fence and Alazani Valley
3. Main Gate of Signaghi with Merlon
4. Rehabilitated Signaghi
5. Church of St. Stepane Khirseli

26 BODBE

St. Nino Convent and Bodbe (Qiziki) Eparchy Episcopacy center is located in 2 km from Signaghi. Cathedral was constructed in IV century AD, on the tomb of St. Nino who introduced Christianity in Georgia. Bodbe Episcopacy was founded in V century by Vakhtang Gorgasali. In VIII-IX centuries the cathedral was remade into a three-nave basilica. The Georgian king Demetre I (1125-1156) played an important role in decoration of the monastery. Bodbe monastery was renovated many times by the Georgian kings. From the end of XV century Bishop of Bodbe was the commander of Kakheti kingdom military and administrative entity. In XVIII century Bodbe also supervised David Gareji monasteries. In the 20-ies of the XIX century Father superior of the monastery, Ioane Makashvili, fundamentally repaired the church, decorated it with paintings and made iconostasis. In 1837 Bodbe monastery was shut down. In 1889 by Decree of the Russian emperor, Alexander III, Bodbe Convent was opened (here served Mother Superior Famar – Tamar Marjanishvili). Here also was arranged boarding school of noble ladies. In 1924 the Bolsheviks closed the monastery. In 1991 the monastery life was restored in Bodbe. One of the biggest shrines of the monastery is miraculous icon of Mother Mary of Iveria.

Large enough shops of icon painting and needle work are functioning under the monastery. Nunns are engaged in the activity of knowledge expansion, prepare new religious service books according to manuscripts.

In the end of 90-ies around the spring of water which emerged under the influence of prayers of St. Nino was constructed tub of water for ritual bath and a small church named after her parents – St. Zabulon and St. Sosana (architect Teimuraz Beridze). A lot of people every day visit this place.

1. St. Nino Convent
2. Pathway and Gates to the Spring of St. Nino
3. Living Cells of Nunns

27 TELAVI AND BATONIS TSIKHE

Telavi is administrative and economic center of Kakheti region. It became a town in VIII-X centuries as the capital of the Kingdom of Rahns and Kakhs. From XII century when David Agmashenebeli annuled the Kingdom of Kakheti and Hereti, Telavi lost its importance and continued development as a small town. From 60-ies of the XVII century Telavi is again the capital of Kakheti Kingdom. From that period to this day Batonis Tsikhe (Master's Frotress), 'Fortress of Vakhvakhishvili', 'Korchibashvili Fortress' and Old Fence have been preserved.

In downtown Telavi is located Batonis Tsikhe (Master's Frotress) — residence of Kakheti with the area of 3 ha. Its territory embraces: the fence (constructed under the king of Kakheti Erekle II in 1753), Royal Palace (constructed in the 60-ies of XVII century by king Archil; in 1865 women's college of St. Nino opened in this building and the Palace was remade into a three-level building; today - Telavi museum), bath (in southern part bathing room and boiler are preserved; walls of the bath were painted), and two churches (Small Church and Church of the Court of Erekle II, built in 1758, the latter being simultaneously a defence facility – it has gun emplacements). To the south-west from thr citadel, in tens of meters there is a big abutment (diameter – 14 m). Up to the forties of the XIX century a big 7,5 m length cannon stood on it.

1. 'Batonis Tsikhe'
2. Sword of Erekle II
   (Exibit of the museum)
3. Palace of Erekle II

28 TSINANDALI

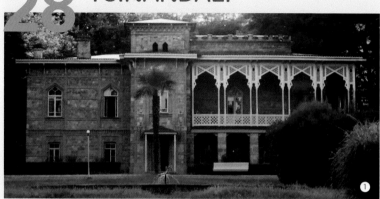

Near Telavi is located the museum of the prominent Georgian poet and public figure, Alexander Chavchavadze (1786-1846). His father, Garsevan Chavchavadze, was the ambassador of the king of Kartli and Kakheti Erekle II to Russia. When Alexander was a small boy he was baptized by the Empress of Russia, Catherine II. Therefore, from his boyhood he had to be in the environment of aristocratic society. European education and way of life can be traced in the estate arranged by Alexander Chavchavadze. He was the first who introduced carriage and grand piano in Georgia. He laid out Tsinandali garden extending to 12 ha and comprising numerous exotic plants of European, Asian and American origin according to the plan of European designers. Alexander Dumas called Tsinandali park Garden of Eden.

Alexander Chavchavadze, his spouse Salome Orbeliani and four children (David, Nino, Ekaterine and Sopio Chavchavadze) were noted for their hospitality. Tsinandali was in various time visited by: Alexander Dumas, French historian Mari-Felicite Brosse, Russian poets Alexander Pushkin, Mikheil Lermontov and Alexander Griboedov.

By introducing European technology of brewing wine Alexander Chavchavadze renewed the millenium-old tradition of production of wine in Georgia. He improved the quality of Kakheti wine and introduced and developed original technologies for production of champagne wines and brandies. Alexander Chavchavadze was the first enologist in Georgia. In Tsinandali he built winery, shop for distillation of vodka and huge underground wine cellar where he placed big vats and opened a shop making barrels. In the wine repository of Tsinandali today is preserved personal collection of wines belonging to Alexander Chavchavadze which included 16 500 bottles of 70 brands of wine.

After demise of Alexander and his spouse, in 1846-1847, Tsinandali estate was managed by their children, at first Nino, later David. On July 4, 1854 Shamil's troops cracked down on Tsinandali Palace. Later David Chavchavadze tried to develop estate of Tsinandali and took a loan from the bank. However, he did not appear to be as successful mamager as his father, and he collected debts. Tsinandali estate was handed over to the Russian government, and lands belonging to the family of Chavchavadze were sold.

In Soviet period Tsinandali was a government residence. From 2007 Silk Road Group purchased Tsinandali estate and restored its museum. It gained the function of a contemporary museum. Part of the museum is used for private or government events. Tsinandali after restoration consists of 4 parts: museum, park, hotel accomodation and wine repository (winery and wine cellar).

1. Museum of A. Chavchavadze (front view)
2. Museum of A. Chavchavadze (side view)
3. European Garden of Tsinandali Palace
4. Wine Repository of Tsinandali

29 IKALTO AND SHUAMTA

Ikalto monastery complex is located in 8 km from Telavi to the North. Monastery was founded in VI century by Holy Father from Assyria, Zenon Ikaltoeli. Arsen Ikaltoeli who arrived from Gelati Academy at the beginning of XII century founded here a center of education – Academy. Monastery complex nowadays consists of 3 churches: main church of Transfiguration of the Saviour, or 'Deity' (VIII-IX centuries) which was constructed on the site of an old church with the tombs of Zenon Ikaltoeli; small Trinity Church with a dome (V century), and one-nave church of All Saints (XII-XIII centuries). Undeviating building of Ikalto Academy has been constructed with cobblestone on the edge of XII-XIII centuries. The first level is a general hall (25m x 9m), the second level consists of 2 rooms. In the ruins of the Academy there are some remnants of scientific and educational articles: basis of cathedra, typical windows with shelves. Like Gelati, in Ikalto Academy education was conducted under Trivium-Quadrivium system. Blacksmith's work, ceramics, viticulture and wine production were also taught. On the territory of the Monastery there are ruins of a dining hall, likewise there are distinct stone remnants of winepress tub and many clay vats.

The Georgian architectural cluster is located in the Telavi region, in the forestland within 7 km distance. It consists of 2 parts: Old Shuamta and New Shuamta. The monastery received its name from its location – it is surrounded from three sides by mountains and has been constructed on the ravine between mountains.

Old Shuamta complex consists of three churches: three-nave Basilica (V century), a dome church of the type of Jvari (cross) church in Mtskheta (VII century), and small dome church (VII century). All three of them have been built with cobblestone, for corners pumice stone has been used. In XVI century Old Shuamta monastery was deserted.

Not far from the Old Shuamta monastery, the spouse of the king of Kakheti Levan II (1518-1574), Tinatin Gurieli, founded New Shuamta monastery – the monastery of Khakhuli the Virgin Mary Convent. There is a legend that before marriage Tinatin Gurieli had a dream of a place with blossoming cornel and she wanted to erect a cathedral there. When Tinatin was brought to Kakheti from Guria by king Levan, they stopped for a rest in Shuamta where Tinatin really saw blossoming cornel, and after marriage she soon launched a construction of a new monastery there. The church was built with bricks and has a form of a cross with a dome and interior paintings. Church wardens' portraits have survived (king Levan, queen Tinatin and their son). The church was renovated by Erekle II. The complex has also bell tower and other fixtures. In New Shuamta a nun queen Tinatin Gurieli is buried having been admitted to nunnery. Here were also laid to rest poet and public figure, Alexander Chavchavadze, and representatives of the noble families of Chavchavadze, Karalashvili, Makashvili and Abdronikashvili.

1. Ikalto Academy (General view)
2. Old Shuamta Complex (General view)
3. New Shuamta (General view)

30 ALAVERDI

Alaverdi monastery and Episcopacy cathedral is located near the hamlet of Alaverdi in Akhmeta region, 20 km from Telavi. Alaverdi Monastery was founded in VI century by St. Father Joseph Alaverdeli who arrived from Assyria (his tomb is the most important deity of the cathedral). Today's cathedral was built on the site of the church of St. George in the beginning of XI century on the Decree of the king of Rahns and Kakhs, Kvirike III (1010-1037), and after that it became the center of Episcopacy. The Father Superior of the monastery simultaneously was Archbishop of Alaverdi and carried the title of Amba Alaverdeli (or the Superior Bishop).

From XVI century Amba Alaverdeli is the main church official in Kakheti and is raised to the degree of Metropolitan. Alaverdi is the word of Arabic origin and means Bestowed by the God. This meaning was associated with fertility and harvest, therefore in those nations with primarily arable farming economy, this name is preserved for several populated settlements.

Alaverdy cathedral is the tallest construction (51 meters) among the Medieval Georgian architectural monuments. It is a cross-type, three arch construction. There are three entrances from three sides. Big space of the cathedral interior (42 m x 26 m) is illuminated by a light from 16 windows in the neck of the dome. Alaverdi has a relatively austere decoration with carving and ornaments generally typical for Kakheti religious monuments. The cathedral is built of cobblestone with internal part covered with pumice stone. The Alaverdi cathedral roof is constructed with glazed blue tiles. There are many instriptions of the walls of the cathedral.

The monastery is surrounded with a fence (XVII century) within which there is a three-level chamber – the residence of a Bishop; brick palace (constructed in 1615 by the potentate of Kakheti, Peiqar-Khan), bath, wine cellar, cells for monks.

Alaverdi has experienced many damages due to hostile invasions and earthquakes. In mid-XVII century Persians remade the Cathedral into a fortress. Its full restoration was made by the kings of Kakheti, Alexander I (1476-1511) and Erekle II (1744-1798). They rehabilitated neck of its dome and renovated the destroyed walls with bricks. Alaverdi was the burial site (XI century, XV-XVIII centuries) of the kings of Kakheti.

In XIX century by Decree of the Synod of the Russian Church Alaverdi like other Georgian churches was whitened with lime. Only in 1966 as a result of a restoration the rich fresco painting of the period of the cathedral foundation (XI c.) and later periods (XV-XVII cc.) was revealed.

Alaverdi cathedral was one of the important centers of Georgian literacy. Here was rewritten one of the oldest Georgian manuscripts – Alaverdi Gospels (1054) which today is kept at the National Center of Manuscripts. On September 27, the day of the Holiday of Universal Exaltation of the Cross, is celebrated the Day of Alaverdi – Alaverdoba. This is a time-honored tradition and is linked to the harvest and stockpiling of agricultural produce and is conducted for the sake of the founder of the cathedral, Joseph Alaverdeli. The worshippers during Alaverdoba come here from various regions to spend the whole night. From its inception, in old times, the holiday lasted three weeks.

1. Alaverdi Monastery (General view from the South)
2. Alaverdi (Interior)
3. St. Georgi Church of Alaverdi (View from South-West)

31 GREMI AND NEKRESI

Medieval fortified town of Gremi, the residence of the kings of Kakheti (1466-1614), is located to the East, 20 km from Telavi and 16 km from Kvareli, 480 meters above the sea level. Gremi used to be not only political but also economic and cultural center of Kakheti. The literacy activity was very active here. It was on the path of caravan ways. As a result of Iranian Shah Abbas I invasion in Kakheti, Gremi was ransacked.

Fortified town area was 50 ha and it consisted of three major parts: Complex of All Angels, Royal Residence and Merchants neighborhood.

Complex of All Angels was isolated by a fence. It had a stone-paved secret exit toward river Intsobi. In the eastern citadel of Gremi is located the church of All Angels having the form of a cross with a dome (built in 1565 by Kakheti king Levan, painting finished in 1577). On the western wall of the interior of the cathedral, church wardens' portraits are represented. The fence of the Cathedral equipped with gun emplacements was at the same time a reinforcement which was rehabilitated by Erekle II. In the Royal residence there were Royal Palaces, a building with a fountain, eight-angle tower, brick royal bath supplied with water through an aqueduct linked with river Lopoti. The whole town was crossed by ceramic pipes of running water. Merchants' neighborhood compiles an indoor market (kulbaks) and a hotel (karvasla). The market was a fenced territory paved with stone with four rows of arched shops (dukani) (overall 30 shops).

Each dukani (area 10 sq.m.) consisted of a room and a veranda open to the courtyard where goods for sale were stocked. Some dukani had a basement. The kulbaks from the East were attached to the corridor-type hotel of 80 meters long (it had 16 rooms each from both sides). In 80-ies of the XX century a local history museum was opened here. On December 12, 1999 religious life was revived in Gremi.

Historical township of Nekresi was located in Kakheti, near the hamlet of Shilda in today's Kvareli region, on the mountain slope. The township was founded by the king of Kartli, Parnajom (II c. BC). In IV century king Mirdat built here a church where Assyrian st. Father Abibos Nekreseli settled in the VI century and Episcopacy Cathedra was founded. From Nekresi the political and cultural influence of the Kartli Kingdom spread to Hereti, mountainous regions of eastern Caucasus and Dagestan.

The Nekresi complex encompasses several monuments the oldest of which is Small Basilica of the second half of IV century (size: 4,6 x 3,8m, one of the first Christian constructions in Georgia). Big three-church Basilica was constructed in the name of Assumption of the Virgin Mary in VII century and was painted in XVI century (in the western part of the southern wall there are portraits of king Levan and his spouse Tinatin under the auspices of whom the paintings were made). And the dome church derides from VIII-IX centuries. From the two-level palace of Nekresi Bishop there are only ruins left. The tower was added to the Palace in XVI century. On the territory of the monastery have also survived remnants of living and farming buildings. Archeological excavations in Nekresi have discovered character signs which in the opinion of the part of scholars are ancient Georgian inscriptions. Nekresi is surrounded by stone fence which used to have entrance from south-west.

Nekresi observes the procedure distinct from all Orthodox churches. Only in this church they slaughter a hog. This tradition stems from one occasion. Nekresi fortress was assulted and surrounded by the Lezghins. When the Georgians felt that difficulties are unbearable, they resorted to a sly prank: they slaughtered all swines available in the fortress, spilled the blood over the fence and dropped the meat. Muslim Lezghins lifted the siege and returned back. So was spared the fortress and the monastery from plunder. After that every November 7 the celebration called Nekresoba is held.

1. Gremi (General view)
2. Nekresi Church of Assumption of the Virgin Mary

32 GURJAANI ALL SAINTS AND KVETARA

Gurjaani Assumption of the Virgin Mary monastery is located near the village of Gurjaani, in the forest, in the Kakhtubani gorge, 2 km from the town of Gurjaani. The pundits of art have an opinion that it was built in VII century. The All Saints of Gurjaani is a complex architectural construction. Three types of building materials have been used to construct a cathedral: cobblestone, pumice stone and brick. This is the only two-dome church in Georgia. In XVII centiry cathedral was painted. In late Medieval centuries it was a burial site of big nobility of the families of Andronikashvili

and Jorjadze. As a result of an invasion of Shah of Iran, Abbas I, the monastery life here ceased and was rivived only in 1822. In 1938 the All Saints was rehabilitated.

Historical fortified town of Kvetara in Kakheti is located in Akhmeta region, on the bank of river Ilto. Kvetara was one of the centers of the principality (later kingdom) of Kakheti. Kartlis Tskhovreba mentions it from mid-XI century, however according to Vakhushti Bagrationi, it should have been founded in almost VIII century. The archeological research proves that this version is true. Kvetara is surrounded by a solid fence constructed from cobblestone and broken stone the walls of which are reinforced by round and square towers. There is an Acropolis on the highest point of the south-east of the fortress in which there used to be a palace and a church. The cross-type church belongs to the first half of X century. It seems to have been a royal court church. The cathedral is unpretentious, without any decorations and ornaments and is roofed with blue tiles.

1. Kvetara (General view)
2. Palace Remnants in Kvetara
3. All Saints of Gurjaani (Interior)
4. All Saints of Gurjaani (General view)

33 DAVID GAREJI MONASTERY COMPOUND

To the south-east from Tbilisi, within 60-70 km distance, in the semi-desert of historical Kakheti, in the rocky mountains of Gareji lies one of the outstanding monastery centers founded in VI century by Holy Father David Garejeli who came from Assyria. At first he settled in the natural cave with his desciple Lukiane, which later became a noted monastery under the name of David's Lavra and a center of Gareji monastery complex.

In the course of time the monastery complex expanded, and today it consists of more than 20 historical monument. These monasteries are: Natlismtsemeli, Chichkhituri, Tetri Senakebi, Dodosrqa, Udabno, Davitis Lavra, Mravaltskaro, Tetri Udabno, Shavi Senakebi, Berebis Mta, Tsintskaro, Gansashori, Sabereebi, Berebis Seri, Satorge, Kotsakhura, Bertubani, Mgvime, Kolagiri, Didi Kvabebi, Patara Kvabebi, Veran-Gareja, Pirukugmari. In later Middle Ages monateries were linked with each other by means of lookout and alarm towers which have survived to our time in ruins. The importance of Gareji has especially risen in XII-XIII centuries when David Agmashenebeli transferred the monastery into a royal ownership with a tax-exempt status. The Monastery enjoyed donations from the Royal family of Bagrationi. The wardens of the Monastery were members of the king's assembly and enjoyed the right to send honorable bounties to the court. In 1424-1745 the monastery was under supervision of Catholicos. However, later it was again transferred to the royal ownership. The monasteries of David Gareji have underwent numerous hostile invasions, but Georgia's potentates revived ransacked monasteries. David Gareji monasteries have created peculiar monastery and construction tradition and their own school of mural painting. Especially brilliant and impressive is painting of the church of Virgin Mary of the XII-XIIIcc. in the cave monastery Bertubani. Rich collection of manuscripts was kept at David Gareji.

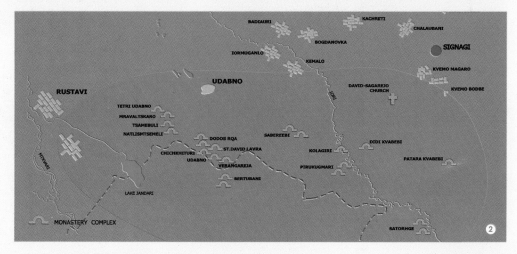

1. David's Lavra
2. Map of David Gareji Monasteries

SAMEGRELO — ZEMO SVANETI

34. Kolkheti National Park

35. River Inguri and Jvari Water Pool

36. Inimitable Summits of Svaneti

37. Ushguli, Tower of Svaneti

38. Dadiani Palace in Zugdidi

39. Martvili (Chkondidi)

40. Nokalakevi

34 KOLKHETI NATIONAL PARK

Kolkheti national park is located in Western Georgia, in the lowlands of Kolkheti, on the coastline of Black sea, in the environs of the town of Poti, 290 km from Tbilisi. It was founded with the aim of conservation of damp landscapes which have international importance and have preserved their pristine appearance that is also related to the preservation of the natural habitat of water and migrant birds. Conservation area is the first site of the Ramsar Convention in Georgia and the Caucasus. Nowadays the Park consists of several wetland (marshy) plots of land and water area of the Black sea. Its total area runs up to 44.3 sq.km with 1/3 of the territory being sea water.

Kolkhety moist territories are relicts of the tropical wetland landscape. These kinds of landscapes several million years ago were present in much vaster territories. From plants we see here species typical for moderate and subtropical zones of wetlands. From moderate belt there are sphagnum bog-mosses (Spagnum imbricatum, palustre, acutiflium), common sundew (Drosera rotundiflora), sedge (Carex lasiocarpa) as well as plants like Pontic rhododendron (Rhododendron ponticum), typical for Alpine zones. On the territory of the park there are remnants of lots of relict and/or endemic species belonging to both wetland and grove forests and coastline dune belt and underwater flora habitats. Two species - yellow hornpoppy and sea daffodil – have been listed in the Red Book. From rare and nearly extinct species should be noted Kolkheti oak (Quercus hartwissiana), wingnuts (Ptero-carya pterocarp), Kolkheti mis-tletoe (Buxus colchica), et al.

Within the territory of Kolkheti national park is also Paliastomi lake which has co-ast origin and several thousand years ago was a gulf of the Black sea. It is separated from the Black sea by several-meter height dune belt. The area of the lake exceeds 18 sq.km, and depth is 3 m. In spite of small sizes, Paliastomi lake is rich with various species of fish. Its diversity is linked to multifaceted changes in the environment. During certain dry years when the lake has drastic drop of water level, sea water trickles down into it.

The territory of the national park is a natural habitat of up to 200 bird species. Among them is Kolkheti pheasant, on the charming attractiveness of which several thousand years ago the civilized world learned from Argonauts.

Damp territories are traditional natural habitats of hundreds of bird species on the path of migration. Millions of birds ‚rest' here in fall and in spring, and in winter a lot of species of birds wait for spring.

In the waters of the Black sea three species of dolphins have their habitat: bottlenose dolphin, common dolphin and porpoise. Here are also Atlantic sturgeon and beluga, mackerel and pink, herring and pike, bullhead and riverside roach. Of 90 species of the fish represented here, at about a half inhabit in salt water and ¼ - in fresh water.

It is possible to visit several important archeological and historical monuments on the territory of Kolkheti national park and in its vicinity. Among them are ancient capital of Lazika – Archeopolis and Christian monuments of Kolkheti – Medieval Martvili Monastery Compound, Monastery of Khobi, Church of Tsaishi and others.

35 RIVER INGURI AND JVARI WATER BASIN

River Inguri flows in Western Georgia on the border of several historical and geographic provinces (Samegrelo, Abkhazia and Svaneti). It's river source is on the watershed of main Kavkasioni mountain range, 2614 meters above the sea level. River flows into the Black sea near the hamlet of Anaklia. It is not distinguished with very big length (213 km), however its parameters of falls and water consumption are impressive and outstanding in Europe. Some segments of Inguri gorge have canyon-like and steep forms where the river reaches big acceleration. In some sectors (right inflow of river Tkheishi) the fall parameter attains 117 meters that makes great impression on a visitor. The catchment area of river Inguri is the third from the point of energy potential in Georgia.

In the middle body of river Inguri, on the margin of Abkhazia and Svaneti mountain ranges, a Jvari water pool was arranged, the dam of which is a unique construction from engineering point of view. Water pool has the biggest depth in the Caucasus and reaches 226 meters.

36 INIMITABLE SUMMITS OF SVANETI (TETNULDI, SHKHARA AND USHBA)

Svaneti is a high-mountain historical and geographic province which is located in the north-western part of the nation, on the southern slope of Kavkasioni mountains, in the catchment area of upper flow of rivers Inguri and Tskhenistskali. The nature of Svaneti, its history and culture is inimitable due to which it is visited by many guests.

The stunner of Svaneti is Central Kavkasioni with several gorgeous summits.

The summit Tetnuldi is located on the Georgian-Russian border, at the source of river Inguri. Its height is 4 853 meters above the sea level. It is the source of several glaciers creating a unique scenery. In the Svan vernacular Tetne means ,white', and Uld is a hypocoristic suffix.

The height of summit Ushba is 4 700 meters above the sea level. It splits into two parts. Northern part is 10 meters higher than the Southern part. Ushba is the-most-difficult-to-climb summit in the Caucasus and Europe. From the point of difficulty to climb the mountain climbers have listed it in 100 most daunting summits in the world. In Svan vernacular, Ushba means ,Stormy tower' proving astounding character of its natural environment. A lot of narratives are related to it most of which tell about tragic relationship between Goddess Dali and a huntsman Betkili.

Shkhara is the highest summit in Georgia. It is located on 5 201 meters above the sea level, on the highest portion of the Central Kavkasioni – the Wall of Bezenghi. Geographers and mountain climbers call it ,Svaneti Alps'. It is covered by glaciers and snow. In Svan vernacular, Shkhara means ,White strip'.

1. Shkhara
2. Ushba
3. Tetnuldi

37 USHGULI, SVANETI TOWER

Ushguli is a marginal area of Upper Svaneti with several hamlets united. It is located on the southern knees of Kavkasioni watershed range of mountains, in the gorge of river Tsaneri (right inflow of river Inguri), 1600-2200 meters above the sea level. By this indicator it is one of the highest human settlements in Europe.

Ushguli is placed in cave-like and well-protected gorge. In the relief of its environs there are both riverside groves and terraces and slant and steep slopes. The average number of precipitations rises to 1200 mm which is very confortable in the existing geographic conditions. On the slopes of northern exposition fir-tree and leafy tree forests are dominant, and on the southern one – second-hand and sub-Alpine meadows.

There are several types of landscapes represented in the vicinity of Ushguli which correspond to well-expressed natural conditions in high belts. Especially effective are landscapes of mixed forests on the lower belt of which ever-green Colchis underbush forest is well represented. It is morphed into a high-mountain forest, then into a sub-Alpine and Alpine meadows, sub-nival and nival landscapes.

There are fragments of a XII century fortress, several churches, more than thirty ancient fortress abodes and cult construction in Ushguli. Some part of fortress abodes are oldest, IX-X century memorial buildings. Ushguli is under protection of UNESCO World Heritage list of memorial buildings.

Svaneti tower is a widespread defensive construction in Svaneti consisting of 4-6 levels topped with two-layer roof. Svaneti tower used to be built with cobblestone and boulders. The overall height of a tower is 20-25 meters. Generally the main entrance to the tower was on the second level. Levels are connected with each other by a moving wooden staircase available in the interior. On the last level of the tower is arranged a weapons platform with gun emplacements. Svaneti tower is a human abode (murkvami) or it is a stand-alone building.

Fortress abode of Svaneti in distinction of tower is lower and more solid and consists of 3 levels. 1 level was used as a living quarter and a barn for livestock. II level was used for economic activity. III level was a loft and was used for defense (for example, Chazhashi Tower).

There is so called Love Tower in Svaneti related to a legend: a daughter of a notable Svan noble had a groom who prepared himself for going to war. A bride vowed that she would not marry and would wait for him return safe and sound. A groom died on the battlefield. A bride did not believe the death of a groom and waited for him. To while away the time during waiting period, a father of the bride built a tower at the beginning of a road where a bride spent the whole life waiting for her beau.

1. Ushguli (General view)
2. Church of the Virgin Mary in Lamaria (Ushguli, Mestia region)
3. 'Love Tower'
4. Ushguli

38 DADIANI PALACE IN ZUGDIDI

Dadiani palace is in downtown Zugdidi. This historical palace and now museum was the residence of Dadiani family – potentates of Samegrelo. The residence of the sovereign was first built by the ruler of Odishi, Levan II Dadiani (1611-1657). Today the historical monument of Dadiani palace consists of palace units constructed under the auspices of the sovereign of Samegrelo, David Dadiani (1813-1853), his spouse, Ekaterine Chavchavadze-Dadiani (1816-1882), and their son Niko Dadiani, as well as court church and botanical garden.

In the 60-ies of the XIX century Ekaterine trusted reconstruction of Dadiani palace to a German architect, Reiss, who used Gothic style while renovating the palace. Two-level palace of Niko Dadiani was built in the 80-ies of the XIX century by a Russian architect, Vasiliev.

The museum of Dadiani palace is the oldest in Georgia. David Dadiani founded personal museum back in 1839 with archeological, numismatic, military and ethnographic rooms. There are more than 40 000 exhibits in the museum today. Among them especially should be mentioned the Shroud of the Virgin Mary, a mask of Napoleon Bonaparte, Shamil's sword, collections of XVIII-XX century European and Georgian painting. In the Gold Fund of the museum there are exhibits of Antique and Middle Age goldsmith's artefacts.

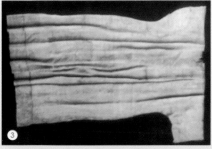

1. Dadiani Palace
2. Niko Dadiani Palace
3. Shroud of the Virgin Mary (Exhibit of Zugdidi museum)
4. Mask of Napoleon Bonaparte (Exhibit of Zugdidi museum)
5. Ekaterine Chavchavadze-Dadiani
6. Niko Dadiani

39 MARTVILI (CHKONDIDI)

The Church of Martvili (Martyrs) is located in the town of Martvili. It was built in the first half of the VII century. In X century, after foundation of Chkondidi Episcopacy, Martvili became the Cathedral of Assumption of the Virgin Mary. The Chkondidi Archbishop was assigned the position of Mtsignobartukhutsesi (Prime Minister) by David Agmashenebeli in 1104.

There was a scriptorium in the monastery. Collection of manuscripts created here is in safe keeping at the National Center of Manuscripts. Martvili church is a construction of earlier cross-dome types of buildings and looks very much like Jvari monastery in Mtskheta. Invasions of Turks and Arabs have damaged it considerably, and due to that, in the X century, the church was substantially overhauled by the king of the Abkhaz, Giorgi II (923-957). New support of the dome was made, outer walls were added, burial vault was leaned to. The painting of the monastery was performed in the XVI-XVII centuries by orders of Odishi rulers. To the north of the main cathedral, on the fence stands three-level minuscule cross-dome type church of Chikvani constructed of cut stones. According to Kartlis Tskhovreba (Georgian Chronicles), the Georgian king, Bagrat IV (1027-1072), was laid to rest in the Martvili monastery.

In ancient times Chkondidi was a hotbed of heathen religious and cult activities. There was a heathen altar on the high hillock – a huge oak (Chkondi) tree. It was a place named after Kapunia, the patron of fertility, reproduction and well-being of the family, who was worshipped by the local population and where local clerics – Chkoindari – sacrificed babies. The first church was arguably built here, on the place where oak tree stood, named after Andrew the First-called who preached Christianity in Samegrelo.

From 2007 the monastery life in Martvili was revived, and the monks' monastery of St. Andrew the First-called and a Convent of St. Nino were founded.

1. The Church of Chikvani and the Cathedral of Martvili (General view)
2. The Images of Church Wardens: Giorgi, Katsia, Otia Chikvani, Sevdia Mikeladze (End of XVII century)
3. Martvili Scenery
4. Cathedral of Martvili (View from South-West)

40 NOKALAKEVI

Nokalakevi was a political center of Colchis (Egrisi) in Antique and early Christian times, the capital of the Kingdom of Lazika (IV-VIII cc.). It is located on the left bank of river Tekhuri, 17 km from the town of Senaki to the North-East (the river encircles the town from three sides). According to the history tradition, the fortress town was first built by Egrisi Eristavi (Duke) Kuji (IV-II cc. BC). The old name of the township – Tsikhegoji (Fortress of Kuji) - is related to him. The Greek sources of later times call this township Archeopolis (in Georgian – Nokalakevi or Old Town, or 'remnants of town'). As some scholars prove, on the exact site of Nokalakevi was situated mythological town of Aya where Jason, Medea and Argonauts have stolen Golden Fleece.

Construction of a fortress town here was determined by military and strategic reasons and plenty of population. Archeopolis was an impregnable fortress in the period of a Great War of Egrisi between Iran and Byzantium (542-562). In 736 the town was seized and pillaged by Arab commander, Marwan ibn-Muhammad (Murvan the Deaf). After that importance of Tsikhegoji went down. In XVI-XIX centuries Nokalakevi was a residence of Odishi sovereigns.

Nokalakevi is surrounded by a fence having 3 km length. Its area is a territory of 19 ha and consists of 3 parts: Lower Town, middle fortress and citadel. The settlement was located on the riverside, garrison was encamped on the plateau, and fortress citadel on the mountain (4 ha). The palace of Egrisi kings (IV c.), three-nave Basilica (V c.), three-nave Basilica remade into a dome church (VI c.), three-level Palace (VI c.), gates with a tower and baths are located on the lower territory of the fortress. There is a Hall Church (VI-VII cc.) in the citadel.

Fortification system of the township is in line with geographic environment. From three sides township was defended by river and steep walls, and from the relatively nature fortified Eastern part 3 fences had been built. The northern part was controlled by a Jikha (fortress) tower.

Both local and imported ceramics, bronze items, necklace, copper and gold coins have been excavated on the territory of the fortress. In Nokalakevi vats and graves of heathen period have been digged where the deceased had coins – Colchis Tetri – stuck in their mouths. Also in Nokalakevi were discovered two baths. One was for the use of a king and nobility, and the other for citizens and garrison. It should be noted that baths were equipped with the system of central heating.

1. Nokalakevi Compound (Interior)
2. Nokalakevi Fence
3. Church of 'Forty Martyrs' (VI c.)
4. Tunnel Leading to the River

KVEMO KARTLI

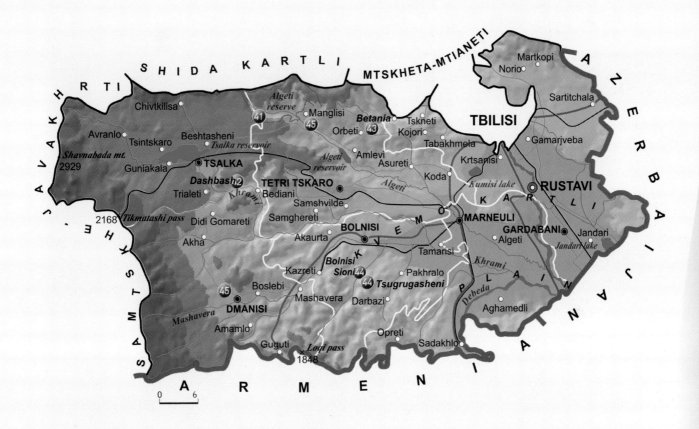

41. Algeti National Park

42. Dashbashi Canyon and River Khrami

43. Betania

44. Bolnisi Sioni and Tsugrugasheni

45. Dmanisi and Manglisi Sioni

41 ALGETI NATIONAL PARK

Algeti National Park is located to the south of Tbilisi, within 60 km distance, in the gorge of river Algeti, 1100-2000 meters above the sea level. It was founded with the status of a sanctuary in the mid-60-ies of the XX century. The main reason of the protected territory is to preserve eastern spruce and Caucasus fir-tree in the extreme eastern advanced post of their extension. In 2007 it was awarded the status of a national park.

The relief of Algeti national park is average mountainous and is distinctly parted. River Algeti with main seasonal inflows is represented in its backbone part. From geological point of view, the territory's structure derives from volcanic flows added by the residue of rocks descending from Quaternary period. Climate is damp and warm characterized by interchange of dry and precipitous spans.

The area of Algeti national park is 6,8 sq. km, most of it being covered with beech, spruce and oak trees. There are groves of fir-trees (Abies nordmanniana), pine trees, hornbeam, ash and birch. There are more than 1600 species of plants on the territory of the park, half of them being herbaceous and more than 1/10 are trees and bush plants. There are also more than 150 medicinal plants, the bulk of which is used both in pharmaceutical industry and by a local population. 3 species of plants are endemic to Georgia.

National park is distinguished also for variety of wildlife. There are several species of predators, amphibians and reptiles, tens of species of birds, etc. From predator mammals stand out brown bear and wolf, pine marten and fox. There are also species included in the Red Book of Georgia among them we note Caucasian partridge and Eastern Imperial Eagle.

There are many historical, cultural and archeological monuments in the Algeti national park and its environs. Most distinguished among them is a Bronze Age Cyclopean Fortress, monastery of the forth century, ancient churches, houses of worship, ruins of the ninth century Kldekari Fortress, chapels, tunnels, eleventh century Fortress Town of Birtvisi. Very near to the Park is Didgori Valley which was the witness of the most important battle in the history of Georgia.

42 DASHBASHI CANYON AND RIVER KHRAMI

Dashbashi canyon is located in south Georgia, in the gorge of river Khrami, between historical and geographic provinces of Trialeti and Kvemo Kartli, 1100-1500 meters above the sea level.

Canyon has been created within volcanic rocks (basalt lava) which construct adjacent Tsalka plateau and Khrami massif. Its several-hundred-meter-height slopes have different tilts in the various parts of the canyon.

Canyon has meridian direction. Its length is 8 km. Within the confines of the canyon prevails moderately damp climate. The annual spread of temperatures is rather high, indicating the continental chatacter of climate. The average temperature in January is 4-6°C, and in July – +16+18°C. The duration of sun light exceeds 9 hours p.m. Volume of precipitation is 700-800 mm, the small portion of which (20%) falls out in winter as snow. In spite of small volumes, sustainable snow blanket is preserved for 3 months.

Dashbashi canyon is distinguished with natural variety and impressive scenery. There are many discharge outlets of underground waters and water- falls on its slopes. We come across both natural caves and those underscored by humans.

Within the frames of the canyon and in its vicinity there are several types of landscapes present - Alluvial fans and plateaus, leafy (beech, mixed hornbeam and oak, and hornbeam) forests and high-mountain steppes, xerophytic plants and derivatives, second-hand meadows and bush forests. Gorge is a natural habitat and reproduction venue for plethora of wildlife species. It is an important geological corridor by means of which many wildlife species of eastern and southern Georgia communicate with each other.

The main artery of Dashbashi canyon is river Khrami. Its gorge is noted with many geographic peculiarities. From the source it flows under the name of Ktsia, however from Tsalka water basin it outflows as Khrami. During millions of years within the volcanic massif it has formed a lot of canyons some of which are impassable and uninhabited. From its source to confluence with Tsalka water basin, river Ktsia is a classical mountain river which boringly flows from the last canyon across the Kvemo Kartli valley. Khrami Canyons are the best objects for educational and scientific tourism on the slopes of which one can vividly see the history of the geological development of the region.

43 BETANIA

The cross-dome type cathedral of Betania is located in the region of Kvemo Kartli, 15 km to the south-west from Tbilisi, in the gorge of river Vere. Betania was considered lost and was discovered anew in the XIX century. To the west of the main cathedral there is a small hall church of St. George erected in 1196 by the father's sister of Queen Tamar, Rusudan. Church was abandoned for a long time, and in mid-XIX century it was cleaned by an artist, Grigori Gagarin, who also revealed a fresco of Bagrationi Royal family (Giorgi III, Tamar, Giorgi IV). In 1894-1896 monk community settled in the monastery again. The outer coverage of the Cathedral has been rehabilitated. Eastern facade and window rims have ornaments. The best specimens of XII-XIII century Georgian mural painting are present here.

There is a figure of Christ Pantokratoros in the arch of the altar, on the walls of the apse there are images of Prophets. On the northern wall there is a mural showing the cicle of crucifixion of the Lord, on the southern wall – scenes from the Old Testament. On the West wall was painted a composition of Doomsday (today preserved only in fragments). The outstanding specimens of secular painting are the portraits of the Royal family depicted on the southern wall – Giorgi III, Queen Tamar and Giorgi IV Lasha. Those paintings were performed in 1206 when Giorgi IV Lasha received benediction of shared crown. Famous Georgian poet and public figure, Grigol Orbeliani, devoted a poem The Face of Queen Tamar at the Church of Betania to this fresco. On the southern wall of the cathedral there is the portrait of a church warden Sumbat Orbeli donned in the attire of a monk and keeping a model of the church in hands. Monastery of Betania was rehabilitated in 2000, extra cells have been built.

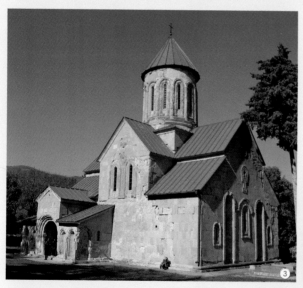

1. Ornaments of Betania
2. Warden Portraits of the Royal Family of Bagrationi (Giorgi IV Lasha, Tamar, Giorgi III)
3. Betania (View from South-East)
4. Betania (General view)

44 BOLNISI SIONI AND TSUGRUGASHENI

Bolnisi Sioni is one of the oldest Christian churches in Georgia. The three-nave Basilica of the Virgin Mary is located in 5 km from the town of Bolnisi. It is distinguished with its architecture and ornaments. In the cavity of the southern entrance to the Cathedral was applied a construction inscription denoting that cathedral was built in 479-494. This inscription is at the same time the oldest specimen of the Georgian script discovered on the territory of Georgia. The inscription tells us that cathedral was built by the first Bishop of Bolnisi, David, during the reign of the king of Kartli, Vakhtang Gorgasali (457-491). The belfry standing by the cathedral was built in XVII century.

The Tsugrugasheni cathedral is located in the historical Kvemo Kartli, on the right side of the expanded gorge of river Poladauri, in a couple of kilometers from Bolnisi Sioni, on the right bank of river Bolnisistskali, on the mountain slope. In the inscriptions of the church are mentioned Giorgi IV Lasha (1210-1223) and a builder of the church, Hasan, son of Arseni. Tsugrugasheni was planned like Betania church, but it is smaller with much higher neck of the dome. The outer form of the construction is stretched from east to west and is placed in the form of slightly prolonged square. The interior space is created from four sleeves of the cross of which only eastern sleeve ends with apse. On the both sides of the altar are placed two-story auxiliary premises which in its first floor have table of oblation and a deacon's closet. From the north the chuch has an annexe presumably added later, a family burial vault. In the construction of the cathedral colour stones were used with extreme subtlety: warm yellowish golden, wine and blue colour stones. The cathedral is lavishly decorated with rich ornaments.

1. The Church Warden Inscription (Bolnisi Sioni, 494)
2. Bolnisi Sioni (View from the East)
3. Tsugrugasheni (General view)
4. Ornaments of the Neck of Tsugrugasheni Dome

45 DMANISI AND MANGLISI SIONI

Dmanisi is a fortified town of Middle Ages. It is located in Kvemo Kartli, at the confluence of rivers Finezauri and Mashavera, 93 kilometers to the south-west from Tbilisi. In historical sources it was first mentioned in IX century while the town was under domination of Arabs and was ruled by Emir. In the 80-ies of the XI century Dmanisi was conquered by the Seljuks. In 1123 David IV Agmashenebeli liberated Dmanisi and turned it into a Royal town that was a reason of its special advantage in XII-XIII centuries. Here passed caravan ways toward Central Asia, operated a mint coining money. In XIV-XV centuries Dmanisi resisted several assaults (Tamerlane, Yakub Khan) causing economic decline and devastation of the town. Dmanisi was often taken by the invaders (Ottomans, Persians).

The town used to be encircled by a high fence built from basalt stone and reinforced by abutment with entrance gates built in from south-west. Within the town the streets were paved with 2,5 m tiles. Inside the fortress there is a three-nave Basilica – Dmanisi Sioni (VI c.) which was attached with richly ornamented gates during the reign of Giorgi IV Lasha (1210-1223). Fortress hosts also a church and a belfry from late feudal times. On the territory of the ruins were discovered: wide tunnel leading down to the river, shops (oil distillery, pottery), baths, encampments, cellars, mosque with a minaret, and madrasah. The dwellings of wealthy Dmanisi residents were decorated with color stones.

The environs of Dmanisi were settled from times immemorial. In 1992 archeologists discovered here the remains of human bodies (lower jaw, teeth). The German paleoanthropologists proved that these remains are 1.800.000 years old. Therefore, these are the remains of the oldest human beings on the Eurasian continent. Scholars created plaster casts of Dmanopithec – a man and a woman were given old Georgian names Zezva and Mzia. These casts are kept in Tbilisi, at the Georgian State Museum.

Manglisi Sioni is an important Georgian architectural monument and one of the oldest Christian centers in Georgia. The first church in Manglisi was built in IV century, and from V century it is a center of Episcopacy. The dates of basic layers of today's cathedral go down to VII century. In 1002 cathedral was renovated. Eastern part of the cathedral, entrance gates and ornamentation of walls belong to XI century. Painting of the dome also belongs to that era. In 1852 the Russian administration whitewashed interior of the cathedral that totally destroyed fresco painting. The fence of the cathedral and a belfry built in it were constructed at that time. There is a trace of Russian architecture in the décor of the cathedral. In the courtyard of the cathedral there are a lot of graves of XVIII-XIX centuries.

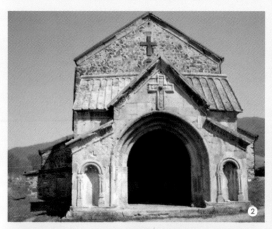

1. Ruins of Dmanisi (General view)
2. Dmanisi Sioni (VI c.) and Entrance Gates (XIII c.)
3. Zezva and Mzia (First Eurasians. Casts from Georgian State Museum)
4. Manglisi Sioni (View from the South)

GURIA

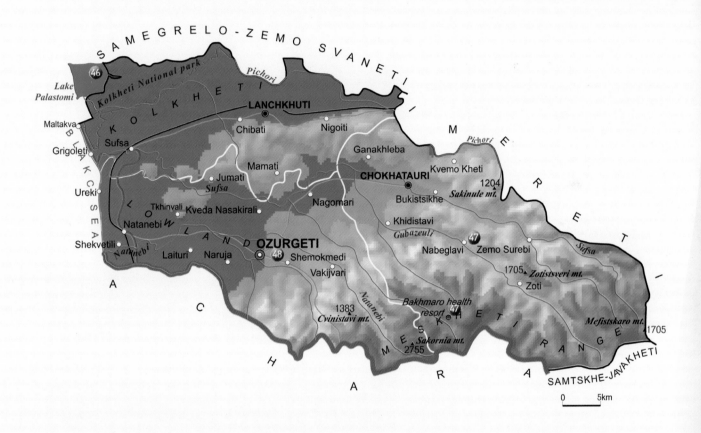

46. Lake Paliastomi

47. Resort of Bakhmaro and Nabeghlavi Mineral Water

48. Shemokmedi Monastery Complex

46 LAKE PALIASTOMI

Lake Paliastomi is located in Western Georgia, on the coastline of Black sea, in the Kolkheti lowland, in the environs of the town of Poti. By its area (18.2 sq. km) it is the third largest lake in Georgia.

The name of the lake is of Greek origin and its direct meaning is Old coast or Old inflow. The oldest gulf of Black sea which turned into a lake was separated from the sea in historical past by 2-km-wide coast dune belt.

Three rivers flow into the lake, and one – river Kaparchina – flows out. The temperature spread of the lake water is 20 degrees. However, it never freezes. In various seasons of the year the lake is typically either rough or has a drastic drop of water level. It relates to strong winds generated on Black sea where its waters reach the lake via special duct (today via strait). The strait connected with Black sea has the width of 150 meters. Due to sea water inflow into the Lake salinity of the Lake is increased 10-fold.

Intense change in salinity has instantly destroyed fish fauna of fresh water which had its habitat here. Some species also linked with the sea had preserved natural habitat. It is known that at the beginning of the last century there were species of catfish and pike represented here which are fully extinct today. Nowadays there are some tens of fish species in the lake of which only carp and mullet are good for commercial catch.

Lake Paliastomi is the major facility of Kolkheti national park.

47 RESORT OF BAKHMARO AND NABEGHLAVI MINERAL WATER

Resort of Bakhmaro is located in Guria, on the western exposition slopes of Ajara-Imereti mountain range, on the latitude of Kobuleti, 2000 meters above the sea level, on the brink of dark coniferous forests and sub-Alpine meadows. Air mass blown from the sea easily reaches here. The height of the venue, high parameters of the direct sun radiation, dark coniferous forest groves and masses of damp air create a unique microclimate for Bakhmaro.

In summertime in Bakhmaro the average temperature is 14°C which makes the place extremely comfortable. It is possible to treat here a lot of diseases. Among them are: respiratory diseases, anemia, neurasthenia, lymph gland inflammation, et al. Here is also a spring of soft mineral water which is widely favored in the whole of Georgia.

In the environs of Bakhmaro, to the south-east from it, 470 meters above the sea level, in the basin of river Gubazouli, is located resort Nabeghlavi. Here is the natural source of a famous mineral water Nabeghlavi. It was discovered in the beginning of last century by the local residents.

Nabeghlavi is known as analogue of Borzhomi. It is a hydrocarbon sodium mineral table drinking water which is used for therapy. Nabeghlavi cures alimentary system, liver (including chronic hepatitis), gall and urine duct system diseases, as well as metabolism disorders (including diabetes). Its application is possible for individual of any age without limitations.

48 SHEMOKMEDI MONASTERY COMPLEX

Middle Age monastery complex in Shemokmedi is located in Guria, on the left bank of river Bzhuzhi, 8 km to the south-west from the town of Ozurgeti, in the hamlet of Shemokmedi. The complex consists of three monument: XVI century bell tower, which was restored in 1831, and two attached cathedrals – XII century Basilica of Deity and a dome church called Zarzma. The latter was constructed by Vakhtang I Gurieli in 1572 to place there Transfiguration

Icon bestowed in XVI century for the purpose of its security. Up to nowadays it is the oldest among the extant Georgian icons and is dated back to 886. As the legend goes, the icon bestowed from Zarzma in Akhaltsikhe was attached to the bull and, presumably, it was supposed to be placed exactly where a bull would stop. That is how this Icon appeared to get to Shemokmedi monastery.

Interior and outer jacket of the church of Our Lord is paved with cut stone and has marble flooring. The church is a three-nave construction without a dome. First it should have been a one-nave building with later annexes of two side naves. At the same time the church was dressed in new jacket and decorated with various color stones in staggered rows. The Shemokmedi monastery was considered the richest monastery and had a rich stock of books. The monastery used to be the burial site of Shemokmedi Bishops and the family of Gurieli.

1. Church of Deity in Shemokmedi (XII c.)
2. Belfry of Shemokmedi
3. Ornaments and Legends of Shemokmedi

SHIDA KARTLI

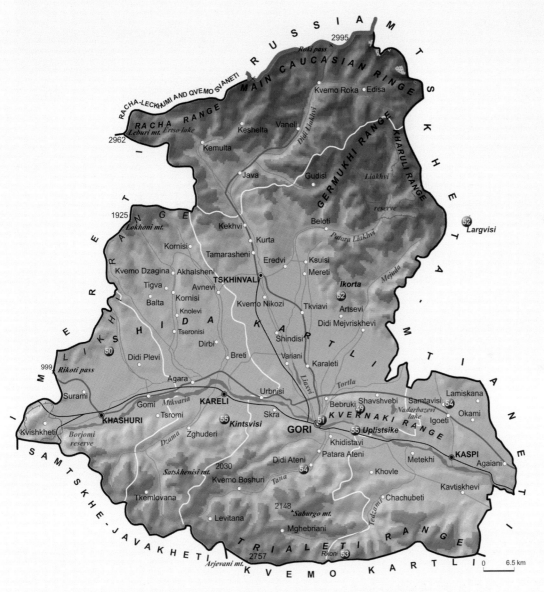

49. Kvernaki Slope (Upland)

50. Likhi Slope

51. Gori Fortress and House Museum of Stalin

52. Ikorta and Largvisi

53. Rkoni

54. Samtavisi and Ateni Sioni

55. Uplistsikhe and Kintsvisi

49 KVERNAKI SLOPE (UPLAND)

Kvernaki low mountain slope which has latitute direction is located in eastern Georgia, 20-80 km from Tbilisi. From the north it extends in parallel with canyon-type gorge of river Mtkvari. The highest summit of the slope is 1114 meters above the sea level. The length of the slope is 70 km and width – 7 km. Its mountain ranges are in distinct difference from each other – the southern part is much more steep and gullied than in the north. The slope is erected by Neogene conglomerates, sandstone and clay.

Kvernaki slope is distinguished with variety of natural conditions. In spite of small scale, lanscape diversity is visible during small movement to another place. Even minute change of exposition brings about change of evaporation that is precondition for development of different species of vegetation. If on southern slopes we see flora typical for semi-desert and arid forests, on western slopes there are thorny shrubberies and degraded hornbeam mixtures, on northern and eastern slopes – oakwood-hornbeam mixtures, and in groves - Tugai vegetation.

Kvernaki slope is one of the formidable old venues of settlements, fortified facilities and historical events in Georgia. The cave town of Uplistsikhe is placed on its slopes, here in 337 king Miriam believed divinity of Christ, here is also artificial cave compound of Shiomgvime belonging to feudal times.

50 LIKHI SLOPE

Likhi Slope is located between western and eastern Georgia, 120 km from Tbilisi. It is an important geographic barrier. It lies on the boundary of moist and dry subtropical areas, catchment areas of rivers flowing to Black and Caspian seas, several historical and geographic provinces. Likhi slope connects also the Greater Kavkasioni range and the Lesser Kavkasioni range. Its highest summit is peak Ribisi located 2471 meters above the sea level. On the western knees of the range is geographic center of Georgia.

Likhi mountain range extends on 100 km and tectonically it consists of several parts. Northern part belongs to Kavkasioni, central part – to Dzirula crystal massif, and southern – to Lesser Kavkasioni. Both in western and in eastern parts of mountains

the volume of precipitation increases in staggering pace, and in the high part (roughly 1200 mm) it nearly doubles.

This situation causes diversity of landscape. Within its borders there are several types of landscapes that are evident when we approach and cross the range.

Likhi slope is noted for wind resources. Here, in the vicinity of peak Sabueti (1248 m) was accounted the highest annual average wind speed in Georgia – 8 m/sec.

Local residents artistically depict the importance of Likhi slope: Likhi slope is mother of Georgia, whose one teat sucks river Mtkvari, and another – river Rioni. Drop of water on its summit splits in two parts – one flows to Black sea, and another half to Caspian sea.

51 GORI FORTRESS AND HOUSE MUSEUM OF STALIN

Historical fortress in Shida Kartli was erected in downtown Gori, on the high rocky hillock. As archeological excavations show, the first fortified settlement here dates to IV-III cc. BC. In historical sources Gori fortress first was mentioned in XII century. Gori fortress had a strategic venue and holding it under control in Middle Ages meant establishment of control over province of Shida Kartli.

Gori fortress was renovated many times, including capital overhaul during the rein of Kartli Wali Rostom (1632-1658). The final face was given the fortress in 1774 when it was renovated by Erekle II. From 1802 Gori fortress became a station of Russian battalion of grenadiers. After that it lost practical importance. Gori fortress was severely damaged by earthquake in 1920.

Fortress was built with cobblestone. In old layers cut stone was also used. The outlines of the fortress are oval. The western part – Tskhrakara – is better preserved, on the southern and eastern parts there are support fences. In southern fence there is an arch gate. On the south-east side of the fortress there are ruins of a small church. The fortress had a tunnel for bringing water and a water pool.

In the downtown of Gori there is a house museum of the founder of the Soviet Union, dictator Joseph Stalin. Museum was opened in 1939; it consists of several parts: 1. One-story two-room building constructed with brick and air brick where Stalin was born and lived until 1883. Rooms maintain family items; 2. Marble protective shelter over this house (architect M. Neprintsev, built in 1937); 3. Two-story Stalin-architecture- style building of museum (architect A. Kurdiani, 1957) with 6 halls where exibits related to Stalin's biography are exposed; 4. Rail car which served Stalin during his travels, including those to International conferences; 5. 6-meter bronze monument of Stalin which was installed in 1952 in downtown Gori, on the square, and was dismantled in 2010 and moved to the courtyard of the museum as an exibit.

1. Gori Fortress (General view from Gorisjvari)
2. House Museum of Stalin
3. House Where Stalin Was Born
4. Stalin's Office (Reconstruction)
5. Personal Armored Rail Car of Stalin

52 IKORTA AND LARGVISI

Ikorta dome cathedral is located on the territory occupied by Russia, 35 km from the town of Tskhinvali. Not far from cathedral there is a family fortress of Ksani rulers. Ikorta cathedral was built by Giorgi III in 1172. By its layout, the dome of a square construction is based on the buttress of an altar and two pillars. Cathedral has a lavish light from 12 windows built in the neck of a dome. Fragments of mural paintings have been preserved in apses, on the northern wall and on the dome. Facades of the cathedral and a neck of the dome are richly ornamented. Ikorta is the earliest specimen of canonic dome church in Kartli of XII-XIII cc. Leaders of anti-Iranian rebellion in Kakheti Bidzina Cholokashvili, Shalva and Elizbar Eristavi of Ksani were laid to rest at Ikorta cathedral.

Largvisi monastery complex is located on the right bank of river Ksani, Akhalgori region, on the territory of Shida Kartli occupied by Russia. According to historical tradition, Largvisi became a town and a church was built in VI century (historical chronicle "The Monument of the eristavi". XIV c.). Largvisi was a center of Tskhradzmiskhevi, there was a fortress there which was the main barrier of Ksani gorge. Famous calligrapher and painter Avgaroz Bandaisdze and his brother Grigol Bandaisdze (XIV-XV cc.) used to work at Largvisi monastery. Many manuscripts were rewritten at the monastery which have survived until our time and nowadays are kept at the National Center of Manuscripts. Largvisi monastery complex is encircled by a fence with towers (XVIII c.). Within the fence there is an inside fortress-citadel. Today's dome cathedral was built on the place of a XIV century church in 1759 by Ksani ruler, David. Cathedral has 2 entrances (from the west and south) and is lavishly lit through windows. On the top of deacon's room a cache is set up. There are gun emplacements. The church overall is less ornamented and the jacket stone of the church is poorly processed.

1. Ikorta (General view)
2. Langvisi Dome Cathedral
3. Langvisi Monastery and Fortress (General view)

53 RKONI

Rkoni monastery complex (VII-XVIII cc.) is located in the vicinity of the village of Chachubeti in Kaspi region, not far from village ruins of Rkoni. The oldest memorial of the complex is church of Virgin Mary (VII c.). In XIII-XIV cc. were built gates of the church of Virgin Mary, chapel, one-nave church of John the Baptist and refectory, tower of Svimon Mesvete; belfry of XVI-XVIII cc., living and utility rooms. Within a distance of 0,5 km from the monastery, on the river Tedzami is a one-span bridge – the best specimen of the bridges of medieval Georgia. Between the monastery and the village ruins is located the fortress of Rkoni (XVII c.). Inside its fence there are remnants of a palace and a church.

Rkoni monastery complex is located in 20 km to the south-west from Kaspi, on the right bank of river Tedzami. In XII-XVIII centuries Rkoni was crossed by important merchant, military and strategic ways connecting Shida Kartli with Javakheti, Trialeti and further, via Armenia, with the Middle East. That facilitated big religious architectural development in Rkoni and its environs.

The core construction of the Rkoni monastery complex is a three-nave Virgin Mary Basilica (VII c.: 18 x 12 m) with the entrance from three sides, deacon's premises, pastophorium. There are small remnants of XII-XVII cc. mural painting. The last renovation of the church was done in 1972-74. From the gates (3,8 x 9,5) and hall-style chapel (second half of the XII century), the remnant paintings of presumably XIII-XIV centuries have been preserved in the chapel. Facades of the chapel are covered with cut stone and adorned with decoration arches and ornaments. The construction included in the complex is a refectory in the north-west from the core church. The main construction dates back to XIII-XIV centuries. Auxiliary premises (5,2x16,6) covered by arrowed arch and based on 6 carrying bends nowadays is severely damaged; the tower of Svimon Mesvete is located in 100 meters to south-west from refectory, on the other side of the river bank. Three levels are currently extant; belfry – to north-west from core church, dates XVII-XVIII centuries, a two-story building. Second level is an eight-arch cylindrical-shaped brick summer pavilion where leads a stair attached from the west side; church of John the Baptist (XIII-XIV cc.) is a hall church (7,3 x 4,3) standing to the south of the core church, in seven meters, on a two-step basement.

Rkoni (Tamar's) bridge is spanned across the river Tedzami within the territory of the monastery complex. The bridge dates back to XII-XIII centuries. Semi-circle 12,5 m bridge is a one-off, monolithic construction elevated on 7,6 m height from the surface of the river. Its width is 2,2 meters. It was built with broken stones in the solid mortar from lime silicate. Abutments of the bridge rest on the natural rocky basement. The bridge is extant in its primary form and is one of the best specimens of fuedal-time bridges in Georgia. Near Rkoni monastery are located a church of St. George in Ikvi and a church of Chachubeti.

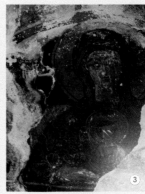

1. One-Span Bridge of Rkoni
2. Rkoni Monastery Complex: Belfry, Church of Virgin Mary, Church of John the Baptist (View from the West)
3. Fresco of Virgin Mary from Rkoni

54 SAMTAVISI AND ATENI SIONI

The XI century dome cathedral of Samtavisi is located in the hamlet of Samtavisi in Kaspi region (one of the legends on the cathedral dates completion of construction works at 1030). Samtavisi is a Bishop cathedral. It was built on the site where the Holy Father, Isidore Samtavneli of Assyria, erected the first cathedral.

The compound is encircled with a fence inside of which, other than main cathedral, are located remnants of the palace of Bishop and a belfry (XVII c.). In the inscription on eastern facade of the cathedral the builder and the first Bishop of the cathedral, Ilarion Kanchaeli, is mentioned. In XV century seriously damaged cathedral was substantially refurbished. It was also renovated in XIX century. In the interior of the cathedral fresco painting has remained only in the altar. Samtavisi is rich with ornaments, decoration compositions. Samtavisi is regarded as the beginning of the new stage of Georgian architecture which evolved in XII-XIII centuries in the Georgian church architecture.

Ateni Sioni is located in 12 km from the town of Gori, near the hamlet of Ateni, on the left bank of river Tani, on the roadside. Cathedral belongs to VIII century and is of a cross-dome tetra-arch type construction (24 x 19 m, height 22 m). It was built with greenish-greyish square-cut sandstone. On the walls of Ateni Sioni cathedral remain unique Georgian inscriptions and postscripts in Asomtavruli mentioning historical

and other individuals, dates and facts. Inscriptions are noteworthy also from language and script points. Interior of the cathedral was fully painted in the second half of XI century. Discriminating manner of painting and technical means, it is possible to identify several artists.

1. Samtavisi (View from North-East)
2. Ateni Sioni (General view)
3. Painting of the Altar (Interior of Samtavisi)
4. Decoration Ornaments of Samtavisi
5. Inscription of Ateni Sioni on Invasion of Arab Commander, Buga-Turk (853)

55 UPLISTSIKHE AND KINTSVISI

Uplistsikhe is located on the left bank of river Mtkvari, 10 km from the town of Gori. It can be detected on the southern slope of Kvernaki mountain range, on the area of 10 ha. Uplistsikhe is the only monument of Antique time in Georgia which nowadays remained above the surface of the ground. Town has streets, squares, water drainage ducts, various constructions, four gates, secret tunnel leading to river Mtkvari, a fence, et al. Today the fortified town is an outdoors museum.

In X-VI centuries BC Uplistsikhe was a fortress of a chieftain (ruler) of the predominant tribe in Shida Kartli. Exactly at that time it was called Uplistsikhe which means Fortified town of a ruler. As the legend goes, Uplistsikhe was built by slaves. Slaves were given a mattock with its blade covered by plain metal while underneath layer made of gold. A slave was supposed to work in a way which would grate plain metal. After that he was granted a gift of freedom and precious metal. Archeological material proves that a human settlement was here even back in XVI-XV cc. BC. In IV c. BC – III c. AD Uplistsikhe was a religious and administrative center. After adopting Christianity as a state religion in Georgia (20-ies of IV c. AD) urban life in Uplistsikhe went down but it still remained a strong fortified town. In X-XIII cc. Uplistsikhe is a buoyant fortified town and its population attains 20 000 residents. Resulting invasion of the Mongols, Uplistsikhe gradually drained of residents.

There are extant portions of halls in the rock of Antique times and Antique theatre of II c. in the remnants of the town. In the central part of the town, in the rock, is evident a big-size, three-nave Basilica (second half of VI c.). In the Northern part of a fortified town stands a three-church Basilica of a crown-prince (second half of X c.). Outside of the church there are barrels for donations. When a child was born in a family, wine was poured into a barrel and when a child turned 16, a barrel was brought to a church and left there. One of the entrances of Uplistsikhe was a secret tunnel. It was cut in the rock and is 41-meter long. During a siege the town was supplied with water and foodstuffs using this tunnel.

Kintsvisi monastery is located in 3 km from the village of Kintsvisi, Kareli region, on one of the highlands of the gorge of river Dzama. The monastery complex consists of churches of St. Nicholas, Virgin Mary, St. George, remnants of a fence and a two-level built-in bell tower. It was founded on the edge of XII-XIII centuries by order of the Royal court. The core building of the complex is the center-dome cathedral of St. Nicholas.

Painting of Kintsvisi performed in the beginning of XII century on special order of Mtsignobartukhutsesi Anton Glonistavisdze, is outstanding. Here are murals of donators (on the northern wall – Giorgi III, Tamar and Lasha Giorgi, as well as Zaza Tsitsishvili-Panaskerteli, on the western wall – Anton Glonistavisdze with the model of a church in his hand), and religious scenes (on the western wall St. Nicholas, Ioane Zedazneli and David Garejeli are portrayed).

A seriously damaged hall church of Virgin Mary dating XII-XIII centuries is located on the riverside of river Dzama, on the slope.

A small hall church of St. George which stands by the western wall of St. Nicholas cathedral was built in the late feudal times (XVI-XVIII cc.).

1. St. Nicholas Cathedral in Kintsvisi
2. Kintsvisi Angel (Mural)
3. Queen Tamar (Kintsvisi mural)
4. Uplistsikhe (General view)

RACHA — LECHKHUMI

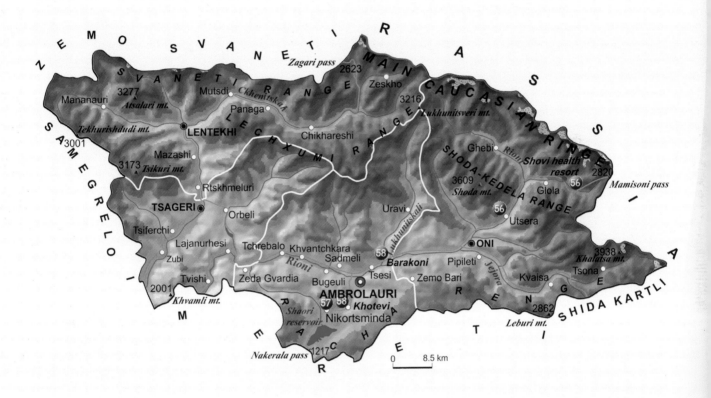

56. Resorts of Racha

57. Nikortsminda

58. Barakoni and Khotevi

56 RESORTS OF RACHA

Racha is the most beautiful corner of Georgia. It is located on the southern plateau of Central Kavkasioni, between Lechkhumi and Racha mountain uplands, in the area of upper flow of river Rioni. The area of Racha is 2.47 thousand sq. km. It was settled from old Stone Age that is proved by more than single archeological monument. Nowadays a number of Racha dwellers constantly go down – during the last decades its number has shrunk by 1/3. It was established that in summer months, at the expense of seasonal re-emigration, population of Racha increases 5-fold.

Racha is distinguished with diversity of natural conditions. From hypsometry point it is spread on nearly 4 km. In geological structure volcanogenic rocks and chalk limestone prevail. Climate is moderately moist and warm. Average temperature in January is 0^0–12^0C, and in July it hovers around $+7,6^0+22^0$C. Volume of precipitation with the increase in height first goes up (from 800 mm to 2000 mm), and in high mountains again goes down. Geological structure and plush precipitation facilitate salinity of underground waters.

Diversity of Racha's natural environment is in direct link with its landscape variety. In a very short range here, sub-nival and nival landscapes of forests typical for Kolkheti lower and middle uplands morph into forests of Caucasian dark coniferous middle mountain, then switch into a high mountain sub-Alpine and Alpine meadows.

Special recreational function in Racha is held by dark coniferous forests, mineral and thermal springs. Thanks to that local resorts have basically a climate spa purpose.

A spa of Shovi located on 1520 meters above the sea level is noted with inimitable landscapes and mineral springs. The average temperature here in July does not top $+16^0$C that is especially important in summertime recreational season. In the vicinity of the spa there are several flowing springs of mineral water (hydrocarbon sodium and potassium mineral water) which are known among the local residents as sour waters. Shovi waters are effectively used to treat bile and urine ducts, while air rich with phytoncides cures respiratory organs.

Resort Utsera is situated on the bank of river Rioni, 1050 meters above the sea level. July temperature attains $+17^0$C, and annual precipitation volume is 1400 mm. Here flows water of two types of salinity. Hydrocarbon sodium and potassium water treats liver and alimentary tract diseases, and water with low salinity is used for baths.

57 NIKORTSMINDA

Nikortsminda is a dome cathedral in Racha, 16 km from Ambrolauri, in the hamlet of Nikortsminda. Cathedral of St. Nicholas of the Racha Eparchy (XI-XIX cc.) according to the donator inscription on the western gate was built by the first king of unified Georgia, Bagrat III in 1010-1014. The southern and western gates were attached in XI century. In 1534 cathedral was refurbished by Imereti king, Bagrat III (1510-1565). Three-story bell tower of Nikortsminda was built in the second half of XIX century. Cathedral has the form of a short-sleeved right-angled cross, five apses. Interior has preserved frescos of XVII century. The jacket of the church is decorated with well-processed stone. The 12-window neck of the dome is shaped with arcade. Cathedral is lavishly adorned with rich ornaments. There is a big multi-figure bas-relief with a plot, multi-figure scene (Second Coming of Christ, Transfiguration, Elevation of the Holy Cross), images of Saints, mythical and real zoomorphic figures. Windows have encircled ornamented decoration.

1. Relief of the Western Pediment 'Elevation of the Holy Cross'
2. Relief of the Southern Pediment 'Second Coming of Christ'
3. Dome of Nikortsminda
4. Nikortsminda (View from the North)

58 BARAKONI AND KHOTEVI

Barakoni is one of the last important monuments in Racha belonging to the Middle Age Georgian dome architecture. Cathedral of the Virgin Mary is located near hamlet of Tsesi in Ambrolauri region. On order of Racha ruler, Rostom, it was built in 1753 by Avtandil Shulavreli. Cathedral was built with cut stone and is richly ornamented. Restoration of cathedral was done in 1991 after it received damage because of earthquake.

Khotevi is a village on the northern knee of Racha plateau, 10 km from the town of Ambrolauri, 1000 meters above the sea level. First mentioned in historical sources in 'Nikortsminda Annals' (XI c.). Thanks to location on the road connecting Imereti and Lower Racha, Khotevi was an advanced merchant point. Russian ambassadors of XVII century, Aleksi Ievlev and Nikifore Tolchanov, mention Khotevi among towns of the country of Imereti. In XIX century Khotevi was a center of the district of Racha. In the village there are remnants of the church of Archangel and ruins of the fortress of XVI-XVII cc. According to the legend on the name of Khotevi, one of the kings of Imereti relocated here a family of prince Tsulukidze who built a fortress. When construction was finished, a king visited the fortress and asked Tsulukidze: "Is there enough space for you at the fortress?" After that it was named Khotevi Fortress stemming from a pun in Georgian meaning enough space (kho-tevi – enough), later giving this name to the whole village. Fortress is today destroyed. Extant part has emplacements. It used to have a fence. Fortress had two floors. Khotevi fortress used to be very strong and impregnable.

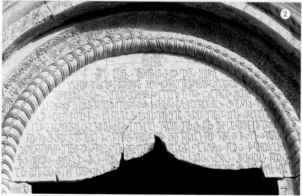

1. Barakoni
2. Donator Inscription on Barakoni Tympanum
3. Khotevi Church of Archangel
4. Khotevi Fortress

MTSKHETA — MTIANETI

59. Kazbeghi National Park

60. Dariali Gorge

61. River Aragvi Gorge

62. Glacier Summit, Ghergheti Glacier and Ghergheti Sameba

63. Mtskheta. Jvari Monastery

64. Svetitskhoveli

65. Samtavro and Shiomgvime

66. Ananuri

67. Fortified Villages in High Mountains – Shatili and Mutso

68. Worship Monuments in the Mountains. Lashari Cross

69. Lomisa

59 KAZBEGHI NATIONAL PARK

Kazbeghi national park is situated in north-east Georgia, on the border with Russia, between the main watershed and side plateau of Kavkasioni, 130 km from Tbilisi. It consists of several territories with overall area of more than 8.7 sq.km. National park expansion is planned by means of linking of its parts. The vertical spread of the national park attains 4 thousand meters and covers both the gorge of river Terek and ecosystems of high mountains.

Territory of national park is noted with diversity of geological structure, active mountain creation and geodynamic processes, lava torrents and canyon-like gorges which are typical for volcanic relief.

Vegetation of the Kazbeghi national park is distinguished with variety and high endemism (1/4). Forests spread on steep slopes and along with high ecological implication create inimitable sceneries. From wood vegetation widely represented are Litvinov birches (Betula litvinovi) and Sosnowski pine-trees (Pinus sosnowski). In the gorge of river Terek there are important spaces of blackthorn vegetation recognized as having important medicinal qualities.

National park is rich with the wildlife species of high mountains among which predators should be mentioned first.

Within the Kazbeghi national park and its environs there are many world-important mountain climbing sites which are known for their complexity and beauty. This region is very rich with many important monuments of historic Georgia among which are lots of early and Middle Age churches, fortress towers, et al. Unmatched are rites and domestic traditions of local residents. There is located also a residence of Catholicos-Patriarch of All Georgia.

60 DARIALI GORGE

Dariali gorge looking like a canyon lies in northern Georgia, in the border belt with Russia, in the area of river Terek. It evolved from Paleozoic granite rocks which are part of the ultimate eastern volcanic process developed in the Central Kavkasioni some 300-400 million years ago. A gorge cut into volcanic rocks is narrow and has steep slopes. Its length is 11 kilometers and relative height exceeds thousand meters.

Within the gorge there are represented several types of landscapes, among them dominating is high-mountain paleoglacier, volcanic and erosion and denudation relief, pine-tree forest, sub-Alpine and Alpine meadows.

Darialani is a Persian word and means Gates of Alans (Ossetians). Georgians mention it under the name of Aragvi Gates, since earlier river Terek was called Aragvi. Other peoples called Dariali Dariela, Gates of Iberia, Gates of Caspian sea, Gates of Sarmatia, Gates of the Gorge and many other names.

For the Caucasus Dariali gorge had ultimate military and geographic importance. It connected North and South Caucasus, however during centuries it was rather difficult transit communication. Landslides were frequent in winter and stone falls used to be the reason of its blocking in summer.

In Dariali Gorge in the first century Georgians erected military fortifications for self-defense from northern tribes. Nowadays the gorge is an object of constant supervision – an automobile road connecting Georgia and Russia was constructed here as well as a gas pipeline laid.

61 RIVER ARAGVI GORGE

River Aragvi gorge is situated to the north of Tbilisi and to the south of the main watershed of Kavkasioni. Its catchment area is 2740 sq.km that comprises 4% of the nation's territory. The fall of the river attains 2700 meters that speaks for great energy potential it has. It is on the 9-th place in the overall volume of potential energy sources. In the basin of river Aragvi there are many rivers under label Aragvi, especially noteworthy for their size are Mtiuleti (White), Gudamakari (Black), Pshavi and Khevsureti Aragvis. Black Aragvi flows into White Aragvi near Pasanauri, and Khevsureti Aragvi into Pshavi Aragvi – near village of Udzilaurta. Pshavi and Mtiuleti Aragvi converge into a single river and flow into Mtkvari near Mtskheta.

River Aragvi gorge is noted with its natural variety. On the perimeter of river flow climate data are rather contradictory. Indicators of average air temperature in July hover from +10 to +23⁰C, and in January – from +10⁰C to 0⁰C, the volume of precipitation swings from 1800 mm to 500 mm. In its catchment area there are 7 types of landscapes that increase perceptional and esthetic value of the gorge.

River Aragvi is characterized by diverse regime of feeding. At its source it gets nourishment from waters of melting snow, in the middle body it gets its feed from melting snow and rain waters, and in the lower flow – from rain and underground waters. Its waters are used by Tbilisi residents, Zhinvali water basin and hydro power plants, Tbilisi water pool (sea), Aragvi gorge settlements and irrigated territories.

Aragvi gorge is distinguished with unique sceneries. It is the most important recreational region for Tbilisi dwellers and guests. Within a very short distance here and in a short time span it is possible to visit assorted natural and ethnographic attractions.

62 GLACIER SUMMIT (KAZBEGHI), GHERGHETI GLACIER AND GHERGHETI SAMEBA (TRINITY)

Glacier summit is located in northern Georgia, on the side plateau of Kavkasioni, on the border with Russia. Its height is 5033 meters. It is the highest summit of eastern Georgia. The local population calls it Bride of the Gorge, neighbor Tusheti residents call it Lion and residents of Pshavi – Ghergheti. For the Russians the summit is known as Kazbek and for the Ossetians – Urskhokhi (Snow Mountain).

The Glacier summit is a dormant volcano that according to the opinion of some scientists last erupted 6 thousand years ago. Here lava torrents flow down in three directions – south, east and north-east. The summit is covered with glaciers which roll down on rather big distance. According to literature sources, the summit was first climbed in 1799 by Father Joseph (Pavlenishvili) who arranged a station here and preached Christianity for two decades. It is also known that in 1868 a famous British mountain climber Douglas Freshwild climbed the summit. Scientific research of glacier summit started in 1923 when the first Georgian expedition took place.

The Ghergheti glacier spreads to the southeastern knee of the glacier summit. Its length is 7,1 km (the longest in Georgia) and area is 11 sq. km. The tongue of the glacier goes down to 2900 meters above the sea level. In its vicinity is situated a high-mountain meteorological station of Kazbeghi which was founded 70 years ago. Here was registered the lowest temperature in Georgia (-42°C) which can be explained by the height of the site (3700 m above the sea level) and the influence of Ghergheti glacier. On the boundary of Ghergheti glacier there is one mythological and one historical monument (Ghergheti Sameba). Mythology tells the story of the Bethlehem cave and Amiran chained at Kavkasioni. As the narrative goes, God has chained Amiran to the rock exactly here and 'Capped him with snowy and icy Ghergheti and Kazbeghi Mountain'.

Ghergheti Sameba (Trinity) is located in Stepantsminda region, on the right bank of river Chkheri (right inflow of river Terek), 1800 meters above the sea level. By its fusion with the landscape and attractive composition, cathedral is the outstanding specimen of the Georgian religious architecture. It is placed on the summit of a high

mountain in a way that can be easily read from river Terek gorge. Ghergheti Sameba is the most important house of worship for the residents of the gorge province and the only dome church in the mountain areas of eastern Georgia. Complex was built on the order of king of Georgia, Giorgi V Brilliant (1318-1346), at time when he enacted a special Collection of Laws 'Dzeglisdeba' for the mountain area residents and facilitated consolidation of Christianity after a century of Mongol domination and ensuing unrest. The architectural complex is encircled with a fence and includes Sameba dome cathedral (20-ies of XIV c.), a belfry (second half of XIV c.), trial chamber (XV c.; according to the old rite of mountains, the council of elders held sessions here and it was a decision-making panel regarding all vital issues in tribe's life). Cathedral was built of andesite rectangular square cut stone. Facades of the two-floor belfry of the cathedral and a neck of the dome are ornamented. As per report of Vakhushti Bagrationi, during hostilities Catholicos's attires and a Cross of St. Nino from Mtskheta were brought for safe-keeping to Ghergheti Sameba.

The Catholicos-Patriarch of All Georgia, Ilia II, has introduced a Ghergheti Sameba celebration on July 16 every year. There is also a big celebration of the Assumption of Virgin Mary here (August 28).

1. Glacier Summit and Ghergheti Sameba
2. Ghergheti Sameba (General view)

63 MTSKHETA. JVARI MONASTERY

Mtskheta was the old capital and political center of the Kingdom of Kartli (IV c. BC – VI c. AD). In the beginning of VI c. when the capital moved to Tbilisi, Mtskheta retained the function of the seat of Kartli Church and from XI century – the spiritual center of the whole Georgia. Until 1811 here was situated the seat of the Head of Georgian Church – the residence of the Georgian Partiarch. Mtskheta is rich with both archeological (Bronze and Stone Ages) and Antique and Christian era historical memorials. Among them it is worth mentioning Armazi – the residence and burial site of the Royals of Kartli from Parnavaziani dynasty (IV c. BC – V c. AD), cathedrals of Jvari (VI c.), Svetitskhoveli (XI c.), Samtavro (XI c.), monasteries of Shiomgvime and Zedazeni (VI c.), fortress of Bebri.

In front of Mtskheta, on the mountain, stands Jvari monastery which became a UNESCO World Heritage Site. The name of the cathedral is related to high wooden cross which was erected on this place by king Mirian. In the second half of VI century the sovereign of Kartly Guaram built a small church beside the cross. This small house of worship is called today Small Jvari Church. On the brink of VI-VII cc. the son of Guaram – sovereign Stepanoz I (586-605) built a big cathedral beside the small one which capped the wooden cross (the abutment of the cross has been preserved until today). After Bolnisi Sioni Jvari cathedral represents a new stage in the development of architectural art. 3 bas-relief images of individuals who masterminded and paid for construction of the church are placed on the eastern façade: in the middle, sovereign Stepanoz genuflecting before Christ; on the left – his brother Demetre with protector angel, on the right – heir apparent of Stepanoz, Adarnase (above him is depicted an angel with widely spread wings and a right hand stretched forward); in front of Adarnase is a child on the knees – his son. All three bas-reliefs have Asomtavruli inscriptions containing names and titles of builders.

Jvari cathedral launched a new stage of the Georgian religious architecture – dome church. In VII century the whole group of similar churches were founded which were close to Mtskheta Jvari in layout and general structure. They are Ateni Sioni, Old Shuamta, Martvili.

1. Mtskheta Jvari (General view)
2. Glorification of the Cross (Bas-relief on the Arch of South Gate)
3. Bas-relief with Image of Sovereign of Kartli, Stepanoz I, the Donator
4. Historic Part of Mtskheta; Armazi Mount, Confluence of Mtkvari and Aragvi (View from Jvari Monastery)

64 SVETITSKHOVELI

Svetitskhoveli, located in the heart of Kartli, in downtown Mtskheta, was built in XI century, is a cathedral and a residence of the Patriarchate. Among the existing today middle-age Georgian Christian cultural monuments Svetitskhoveli is the greatest. The first hall church was built here as early as IV c. ruins of which are visible in the interior of the cathedral, under glass flooring. Inside the cathedral is basilica built by the king of Kartli, Vakhtang Gorgasali, in V century. Today's cathedral was built on order of Catholicos-Patriarch of Mtskheta, Melkisedek, in 1010-1029 by architect Arsukisdze. A legend floated that when construction of cathedral was finished, the architect's right hand was severed since he prevailed and overtook his teacher in architectural mastership. Svetitskhoveli is considered to have triggered a starting point of the whole direction in the Georgian Middle Age central-dome architecture.

Svetitskhoveli underwent many restorations. In the reign of the king of Georgia, Alexander I (XV c.), dome neck and façade were restored, some bas-relief images changed their places. Fresco painting of the Cathedral belongs to later time (for the most part, XVI-XVII cc.). Svetitskhoveli is surrounded by a two-tier fence with combat path, gun emplacements and loopholes for pelting stones which were built by the king of Kartli and Kakheti, Erekle II in 1787. Cylinder and 2 corner towers are built-in in the fence. In the southern wall of the fence is located entrance gate. On the western side are a belfry and a gate of XI c. In the south-eastern part of Svetitskhoveli courtyard is a palace of Catholicos-Patriarch, Anton II (1788-1811).

1. Svetitskhoveli (General View from Jvari Monastery)
2. Svetitskhoveli (View from north-west)
3. Relief Image of Donator
4. Sun Watch
5. Hand of the Architect of Svetitskhoveli
6. Mural Painting of the South Wall of Svetitskhoveli

65 SAMTAVRO AND SHIOMGVIME

Samtavro is a complex of XI century located in the downtown Mtskheta. It consists of a big Episcopacy cathedral, St. Nino church, belfry, fence, tower and living and service quarters built later. According to historical reports, in VI-VIII cc. this was a residence of the ruling prince of Kartli wherefrom comes its name – Samtavro (Principality). Here lived Nino who arrived to Georgia to preach Christianity. Today it is a convent.

Big cathedral is a cross-dome construction (27 x 23 m) with south, north and west annexes. As a result of an earthquake in 1283, a dome collapsed and was restored on the edge of XII-XIV cc. In the end of XVII c., in the second half of XIX centuries and in 1974 cathedral was fundamentally renovated. In the south-western corner of the cathedral there are gravesites of the first Christian king of Georgia, Mirian, and queen Nana. Monument of the gravesite has been renewed in XIX century. Painting of the cathedral belongs to XVII century.

Church of St. Nino is a small-scale dome construction (6,2 x 3,9 m). It stands to the east of the big cathedral. It was built by king Mirian on this blackberry bush area where Nino settled first. Interior of the church is painted with compositions on the life of St. Nino and other themes. Painting is primitive and late.

Three-story belfry (4,7 x 5,8 m) was built in XV-XVI cc. with square cut yellowish-grayish sandstone, in twenty meters to the north-west from the cathedral, on the elevated platform.

From old fence remained a damaged cylindrical tower standing in the south-western corner of the courtyard, on the height (today living quarters of the convent). It was built in XVIII c. Existing fence belongs to XIX century.

Shiomgvime monastic complex was one of the outstanding religious and cultural centers in the feudal time Georgia. It is located some 40 km from Tbilisi, in Mtskheta region, on the left bank of river Mtkvari. It was founded in the second half of VI century by one of the Assyrian preachers named Shio. As the sources tell us, Shio spent the last years of his life in dark and deep cave and after demise, according to his will, he was buried there. That is where the name comes from – Shios mgvime (Cave of Shio). His grave in Shiomgvime is a sacred place. Shiomgvime monastic complex includes: dome church of John the Baptist (middle of VI c.), the Upper church (XI-XII cc.), refectory (XII c.) and a chapel near monastery (XII c.). Water was supplied to monastery from the hamlet of Skhaltbi. Shiomgvime was a hotbed of culture and education in medieval Georgia. The library of Shiomgvime kept a rich collection of manuscripts. In Tbilisi the monastery held vending booths and bred livestock for sale. It enjoyed privilege and was exempt from any court (partly), Eparchy and state taxes. From VI century up to the beginning of XII century Shiomgvime was in the direct supervision of Catholicos-Patriarch. David Agmashenebeli turned it into a Royal ownership. In XIII-XVIII centuries political and economic position of Shiomgvime went down. In XIX-XX centuries Shiomgvime was fundamentally restored.

1. Samtavro Episcopacy Cathedral
2. Samtavro Church of St. Nino
3. Shiomgvime (General view)

66 ANANURI

Ananuri complex (cathedral and fortified town – XVI-XVII cc.) is located in Dusheti region, about 23 km from the town of Dusheti, in river Aragvi gorge, on the coast of Zhinvali water basin. Ananuri used to be a residence of Aragvi rulers (up to 1743) and consisted of Upper (XVII c.) and Lower (XVIII c.) fortresses and secular and religious constructions included in it: pyramid-type five-floor tower of Ananuri citadel (XIV-XV cc.), one-nave church Mkurnali (Healer) (XVI-XVII cc.), dome cathedral of Deity (middle of XVII c.) and main cathedral (in 1689 was built by Kaikhosro Bagsarashvili by order of Aragvi ruler). Fresco painting of the main cathedral today is rather damaged. Doors and windows are trimmed by ornamented bas-relief compositions.

Citadel of Ananuri fortress consists of several towers of which only southern and western central towers are quadrangular, the rest of them have cylinder form. Walls of the fortress at first did not exceed 5-6 meters, but later they were added 2-3 meters. All towers of the citadel are for combat but are also equipped with living elements. The biggest and most distinguished is Sheupovari (Audacious). It has seven levels. It was equipped with gun emplacements, cannons and loopholes for pelting stones. Ananuri fortress had its own running water from western wall which was then collected in the repositories. Big strategic importance of Ananuri fortress is proved by the fact that in 1795 after defeat in Krtsanisi battle king Erekle II found refuge in Ananuri. Today Ananuri is one of the best preserved historical and cultural monuments.

1. Ananuri Complex
2. Donator Relief
3. Ornaments of Eastern Façade
4. Ananuri and Zhinvali Water Pool
5. Fresco Painting of Ananuri

67 FORTIFIED VILLAGES — SHATILI AND MUTSO

The hamlet of Shatili is located in Upper Khevsureti, 15 km from the town of Dusheti, 1000 m above the sea level. Peppered on the rock, Khevsureti towers were fortified living quarters which defended from enimy invasions not only a hamlet but played the role of northern barrier for the whole of Georgia and defended the nation from intrusions of nomadic tribes.

Fortified houses are attached to each other and thus they create a unified defence wall. Buildings are arranged as terraces. They have flat roofing. Between houses, across the whole village is paved a stone stairway. The hamlet of Shatili consists of several neighborhoods (Anatori, Kavchi, Middle Hamlet, Zenubani) which are connected with each other by narrow passages. At the entrance to the hamlet is a stand-alone building called Sapikhvno – a one-story building where male population of the hamlet used to assemble for making decisions on diverse issues and for discussions.

Mutso is the oldest fortified village of the Upper Khevsureti in the middle of the gorge of river Ardoti. It ceased to exist in the 20-ies of XIX century after invasion of Shamil's warriors. Village is located on three terraces and is built of slate. In the middle of the terrace is situated a stable Brolis Kalo. Also there is an icon of St. George and lookout tower. Fortress houses are 4-6-story buildings. A barn is on the first level, a sheepfold on the second, living quarters on the third and fourth floors. Upper levels were used as a stockroom and a closet.

1. Shatili (General view)
2. St. George Icon of Brolis Kalo in Mutso
3. Mutso (General view)

68 WORSHIP MONUMENTS IN THE MOUNTAINS. LASHARI CROSS

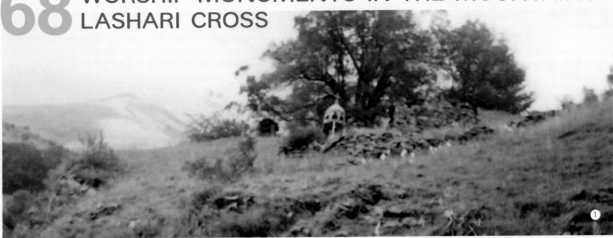

Lashari Cross house of worship is located in Down Pshavi, in the upper body of river Aragvi, on the right bank, rather far from resident area, between districts of Khoshara and Tsitelaurta, on the so called Khmelgori, or Lashari Gori, and occupies the space of 0.75 hectares. The territory of the worship is surrounded by a stone fence in the grove. Not far from the fence is Lashari worship site – a construction with a dome buttressed on four columns built with basalt and roofed with tin plate.

Joint house of worship for 12 main districts of Pshavi is placed here – a warrior deity Lashari and deity of cure and reproduction - queen Tamar Akim. The cult of Lashari besides Pshavi was also spread in Tusheti, Khevsureti and among adjacent districts of valley and North Caucasus mountain residents. Lashari Cross was considered one of the richest deities which owned many donated treasures (including those of Georgian kings), estates, vineyards in Kakheti. As Vakhushti Bagrationi conveys, Lashari Cross was founded by the king of Georgia, Giorgi Lasha (1210-1223). However functionally, by linguistic and ethnographic data, Lashari was a heathen deity which

merged with the cult of Messiah's Sword, a liberator, commander of troops.

The rite of Lasharoba begins with stabbing of sacrificed calves (this is a direct function of Khevisberi – the Elder in the gorge), after that follow prayers. New Year congratulators dance Perkhuli. In the evening worshippers go to the bank of Aragvi where they continue their binge the whole night. Next morning they climb to the Icon of Queen Tamar.

In front of Lashari Cross, on the summit of a forest mountain, stands the Icon of Queen Tamar surrounded by a fence. Inside the fence is a holy grove – its abuse means a bane to oneself. To the east of the fence a slope is smoothed and supported by a stone levee. From the levee protrude benches for worshippers. To the south of the fence there is a stone house for banners of archpriests, there are also clay vats with church wine. A house for distilling beer stands by. There are 2 belfries within the fence: one is made of stone and plastered with lime, with a dome, with two huge bells hanging. The second is made of wood. Near the entrance gate in the fence icons are placed and an altar is fixed.

1. Khmelgori (General view)
2. Prayer Niche of Lashari
3. Lashari Chapel (Interior)
4. Khevisberi at the Ritual of Mercy

69 LOMISA

Church of St. George of Lomisa (VIII-IX cc.) and a chapel are located on the watershed mountain of rivers Ksani and Aragvi. The construction is a simple three-church basilica. Around the cathedral there are extant ruins of verious buildings. In times of pagan worship Lomisa (the name is related to a bull whose cult was merged with the cult of moon – horns of a bull and half-moon) was allegedly a moon-worship temple. Afterwords a Christian church was built on the venue of a heathen temple. Lomisa was the main place of worship for the population of mountain area and Ksani gorge. Gatherings of the Council of Elders decided here political and legal issues.

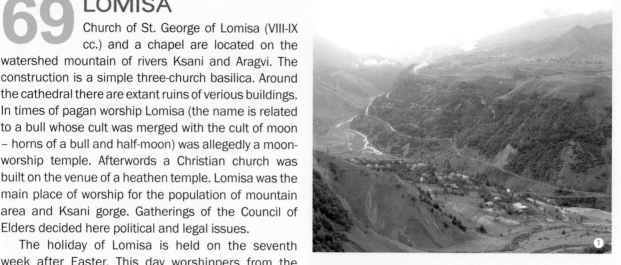

The holiday of Lomisa is held on the seventh week after Easter. This day worshippers from the whole of east Georgia gather at the hamlet of Mleta. Archpriests carry out a banner and accompanied by singing Perkhisa take it up the mountain where celebration with sacrifice takes place. St. George of Lomisa was recoursed to when child was born, or light of day, or welcom to a harvest were celebrated. In the name of Lomisa they worship the siperior cross attached to a wooden flagpole with balls fastened to its four ends (solar symbol). According to the legend, Lomisa was a warrior, he sat on a scarlet horse with a whip in his hand that helped him to sear evil. The cult of Lomisa seems to have already been dispersed in Georgia back in the Bronse Age. In Christian era it was linked with St. George.

1. **View of Aragvi Gorge from Lomisa Mountain**
2. **Lomisa Chapel**
3. **Lomisa Church of St. George**
4. **Worship Niche**

SAMTSKHE — JAVAKHETI

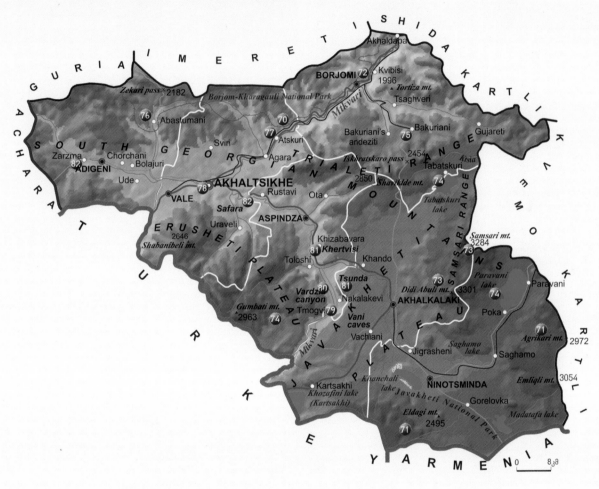

70 BORJOMI—KHARAGAULI NATIONAL PARK

Borjomi-Kharagauli National Park by its status is the first protected area in the Caucasus. It was set up in the end of XX century and by occupied area (more than 600 sq. km) is one of the largest protected territories in Europe. It is located in the central part of Georgia, to the west from Tbilisi within the distance of 140 km.

National park is situated on the brink of several physical geographic and historical geographic provinces that determine not only its natural but also ethnographic importance. Within its confines and in nearest vicinity are represented oak groves of Kolkheti forest of middle-range mountain, oak-hornbeam groves, beech groves, hornbeam-beech groves, beech-dark coniferous and upland forest landscapes. Thanks to this it is the most important geo-ecological knot in

the Caucasus and a substantial link in shaping up of a network of preserved territories in the region.

On the territory of the Borjomi-Kharagauli national park distribution of vegetation is based on the extension of warm and moist climate. In the northern and western parts of it volume of precipitation is 1000 mm, and in the eastern and southern - twice as less. Such share of precipitation is the cause of contrasting natural conditions and ultimately swift change of diverse sceneries.

Change of landscapes along with distribution of precipitation is noteworthy also with change of height and exposition. Relative height of the territory of national park attains 1500 meters. Here leafy forests are morphed into mixed, then beech and later high-mountain forests. Sub-Alpine and Alpine vegetation is widely spread here and it is possible to see it by moving to a small distance.

On the territory of the national park we come across such species of vegetation as follows: chestnut, Kolkheti oak, yew, pine and fir. From wildlife species are important Caucasian noble red deer (Cervus elaphus), roe deer (Capreolus capreolus), mountain eagle (Aquila chrysaetus fulva), eagle (Gyps fulvus fulvus), griffon-vulture (Aegypius monachus) and Caucasian black cock.

National park is well arranged for various types of tourism. There are Borjomi mineral water springs, mountain skiing resort of Bakuriani, Bronze and Antique era monuments, IX-X century several famous churches and fortifications near it.

71 PROTECTED TERRITORIES OF JAVAKHETI

Javakheti is a part of Georgian high-mountain area of volcanic origin between Armenia and Turkey. Its ecosystem with its mountain steppes, sub-Alpine bush forests and Alpine meadows, relict sub-Alpine forest copses, wetland vegetation and tens of endemic species is one of the unique areas in the eco-region of the Caucasus.

Special international importance of Javakheti is related to the existence of deeply moist territories on the highland mountains above the sea level, which are a migration hub for birds of Europe, Asia and Africa. According to the International environment protection legislation, Javakheti's highly damp territories belong to the site of Ramsar Convention.

Protected territories of Javakheti are the result of a first trans-border ecological cooperation in the Caucasus. Its formation in Georgia was fulfilled for the first time on the basis of European experience and methodology of landscape planning. Based on the conclusions on landscape planning it is possible to create one national park, 5 sanctuaries, one protected landscape and natural memorial.

On the uplands of Javakheti highly moist territories are represented as lakes of volcanic origin and marshes which evolved resulting eutrophication of lake water in geological eras. From lakes should be mentioned Kartsakhi (on the border with Turkey), Khanchali, Madatapa, Bugdasheni, Sagamo, Paravani and Tabatskuri.

In the area of protected territories 275 species of birds are accounted for that is ¾ of the bird populations of Georgia. Bird populations of the mountain area of Javakheti are represented with at least 225 permanent species and roughly 50 species are rare or periodic inhabitants of the given territory.

The region is very rich with natural and historical memorials. Many national parks and sanctuaries, world-important Vardzia monastery complex and Khertvisi fortress are located not far from Javakhety protected territories.

Borjomi gorge is located in the central part of Georgia, between Trialeti and Likhi medium-size mountain plateaus, 140 km from Tbilisi. Here is the confluence point of historical and geographic provinces – Shida Kartli, Imereti, Tori and Meskheti.

Borjomi gorge accompanies river Mtkvari for 60 km. Within its confines are knees of Likhi, Ajara-Imereti and Trialeti plateaus with their relative height attaining 1,5 km. In the environs of the town of Borjomi the gorge has a canyon-like form which was created as a result of a 'break in' of Bakuriani lava slide.

Borjomi gorge is represented in the nearest vicinity of eastern part of Akhaltsikhe cave and western part of Shida Kartli which are distinguished for continental climate (negative temperature in winter) in the Georgian plain between mountain ranges. From Likhi medium-sized mountains damp masses of Black sea winds easily 'slide' here that is the reason of 1,5-fold precipitation compared with the adjacent territories. The special recreational power of the gorge stems from micro-climate peculiarities and dark coniferous forests.

Borjomi gorge has a unique beauty that is related to diversity of natural environment. Here within the distance of several kilometers spruce and fir groves switch to pine, mixed, leafy and alder groves, thorny bushes and steppe vegetation. There are many resorts in Borjomi gorge where holiday-makers spend vacations both in summer and in winter. Not far from the gorge is located world famous mountain and skiing resort of Bakuriani.

Borjomi gorge is witness of numerous historical perturbations. There are human settlements there dating thousands of years, however, due to repeated invasions, in XVIII century it became deserted. Later on it was settled again that is related to the re-discovery of mineral waters. Nowadays the gorge is famous in the Caucasus and Europe for its mineral waters and spa resorts.

Borjomi mineral water with its curing qualities is known in the world as the Queen of mineral waters. It is a hydrocarbon sodium water with very high salinity. From XIX century it became very popular after the Russian Emperor's family built countryside residence palace here. Borjomi mineral water is used to treat chronic gastritis and enterocolitis, diseases of alimentary tract, diabetes, liver and metabolism.

73 JAVAKHETI VOLCANOES

Javakheti volcanic plateau is located in Southern Georgia. It was created by lava slides which flew from slopes of meridian-direction Samsari plateau. There are many volcanic cones on this slope, among them distinguished by scale and beauty are Didi Abuli, Samsari and Tavkvetila.

Didi Abuli is located on 3305 meters above the sea level, in the Southern part of Samsari slope. It was frozen in Quoternary period that is proved by moraines, cirques and small lakes. There is a different opinion on the volcanic action of Didi Abuli. Some scientists think that it should have a status of active volcano. Such position relates to its name and popular sayings. Allegedly, smoke was puffing from the mountain and that is why local population mentioned it as 'smoked' mountain. In spite of this, until now Didi Abuli is deemed a dormant volcano since it is presumed that its last eruption happened only 10-12 thousand years ago.

Samsari Volcanic Cone is located in the central part of the slope, 3285 meters above the sea level. Diameter of its crater attains 3 km on the bottom of which there are several small lakes.

Tavkvetili is located on 2583 meters above the sea level, in the Northern part of Samsari slope. Its name descends from its shape, as volcanic cone is well portrayed. To the west from it is lake Tabatskuri of volcanic origin distinguished in Georgia for its volume of water.

74 RIVER MTKVARI AND VARDZIA CANYON. PARAVANI AND TABATSKURI

Mtkvari is the mother of Georgian rivers, but by many indicators (length, volume of water, energy potential) it is behind other rivers. It flows across the territories of several historical and geographic provinces of southern and eastern Georgia and large urban settlements thanks to which it played a role of important transit artery in the course of centuries.

Mtkvari is the biggest river in South Caucasus. Its overall length is 1200 km and its catchment area attains 200 thousand sq. km. Such tributaries as Paravani (near Khertvisi), Potskhovi (near Akhaltsikhe), Liakhvi (near Gori), Aragvi (near Mtskheta), Khrami, Iori and Alazani (near Georgia-Azerbaijan border), Araks (on the territory of Azerbaijan) and others flow into Mtkvari.

It flows into Georgia near Vardzia, in the roughly upright, canyon-like gorge. Canyon has been shaped between volcanic mountains of Erusheti and Javakheti volcanic upland. Its depth near hamlet of Apnia is 500 meters. From here up to the fortress of Tmogvi opens gorgeous panorama.

Among the Georgian lakes the biggest by area is Paravani lake, by water volume – Tabatskuri, by depth – Ritsa, and lake Paliastomi is noted for diversity of species.

Paravani is located in southern Georgia, on the volcanic plateau of Javakheti, between Abuli-Samsari and Javakheti slopes, 2073 meters above the sea level. Lake is outflowing. From it flows river Paravani or Javakheti Mtkvari. It gets its feed basically from underground and snow-melting waters. Underground water determines its temperature regime, that is why temperature of the lake water is always 1-2⁰C higher than air temperature of the adjacent territory.

Big volume of Tabatskuri lake is caused by its surface area (14.2 sq. km) and depth (40 m). Like Paravani lake, it is a high mountain lake and is located on 1991 meters above the sea level, in southern Georgia, between Abuli-Samsari and Trialeti slopes. The lake mainly gets feed from snow-melting waters due to which the spread of the water level hovers around 2 meters. Temperature of its water even in summer months do not exceed +15⁰C. Cold water is a good habitat for breeding trout which is caught in big volumes.

75 BAKURIANI

Bakuriani is a mountain ski resort which is located on the northern knees of Trialeti Plateau, in the gorge of river Bakurianistskali, 1700 meters above the sea level.

Hamlet of Bakuriani expands on the bottom of its namesake valley which has been shaped by volcanic rocks. It is distinguished among mountain resorts of Georgia for duration of sunlight attaining 2100 hours per year. Adjecent slopes of the valley are guised with mixed and dark coniferous forests that increase its resort and recreational aptness. In its vicinity there are three types of landscapes among which beech and dark coniferous forests and sub-Alpine meadows are worth to mention.

Bakuriani is outstanding focal point of mountain ski sport in Georgia which is related to favorable climate conditions. Winter here is long, cold and snowy. Average temperature in January is -7°C and in July - +15°C. Average annual volume of precipitation does not exceed 750 mm, but its basic part (1/3) goes for snow. Snow cover usually holds for 5 months that is distinguishing it from other ski resorts of Georgia. Average thikness of snow cover is 64 sm that is precondition for development of winter sports. There are several functioning ski tracks and technically equipped ski-jumps here.

On the border of Bakuriani is located a botanical garden set up at the beginning of last century. There are some 1500 species of Alpine, moderate belt of mountain system, Kavkasioni and exotic plants. Bakuriani is located near Borjomi-Kharagauli and Javakheti protected territories. Passage to Javakheti is possible through Tskhratskaro mountain range (2454 m) wherefrom opens up a gorgeous panorama of Kavkasioni as well as a plain between mountains of Georgia and volcanic plateau.

76 ABASTUMANI

Abastumani is known in the world for its astro-physics observatory in the mountains. It was founded in the 30-ies of last century on the outskirts of Abastumani. Observatory is situated 1650 meters above the sea level where atmosphere is characterized by very high transparency.

Abastumani is a mountain-climate resort which is located in southern Georgia, on the southern knee of the Ajara-Imereti mountain range, 260 km from Tbilisi, 1800-1840 meters above the sea level. Duration of sun light exceeds 3 thousand hours that is a very high indicator.

Resort is distinguished for sound air related to dark coniferous forests. It is a focal point for treatment of tuberculosis in the Caucasus. In Abastumani it is possible to cure practically any phaze of lung tuberculosis. There are also springs of medicinal thermo-mineral water with temperature surpassing +40°C. These waters were used for the treatment of joints from times immemorial.

In the vicinity of Abastumani is located Borjomi-Kharagauli national park, petrified flora of Goderdzi plateau, several resorts and tens of historical and cultural attractions of national importance.

1. Abastumani Astro-physics Observatory
2. Abastumani (View from Kanobili mountain)
3. Altar of New Zarzma (Artist M. Nesterov)
4. Abastumani Church of New Zarzma (1902)

77 CHURCH OF VIRGIN MARY AND FORTRESS IN ATSKURI

Atskuri was a political and religious center in the medieval southern Georgia. Today's hamlet of Atskuri (old name – Sosangeti) is located in 30 km from the town of Borjomi, and in 22 km from Akhaltsikhe. The first cathedral on the territory of the hamlet was allegedly built at the beginning of VII century. At the beginning of IX century here already existed Episcopacy cathedral. And in XI century in Atskuri was built cathedral of Virgin Mary. It was the biggest cathedral by space in the middle-aged Georgia. In XIII-XIV centuries sovereigns of Samtskhe, atabags from Jakeli family renovated the church. However, earthquakes and invasions of enimies damaged the cathedral considerably. The final destruction happened at the ending of the Ottomans' domination. A dome, an arch of the dome neck and the walls of the cathedral are demolished. Famous educationalists conducted their activities in Atskuri, such as Giorgi Matskvereli (IX-X cc.), Gabriel Kotai (XI c.), Ioakime and Jeremiah Matskvereli (XVI c.).

Near the cathedral is located Atskuri fortress which is a concomitant of the cathedral of Virgin Mary. This fortified facility guarded Borjomi gorge from the south. From 1579 the fortress was included in the vilayet of Cildir. In 1770 the attempt to conquer it by the army of Georgians and Russians appeared to be abortive. As a result of 1829 Adrianopolis peace accord, the Ottoman empire ceded this fortress along with the region of Samtskhe to the Russian Empire.

Atskuri fortress was built on the inaccessible rock that specially increased its ability of defence. Entrance to the fortress was possible through the narrow tunnel cut out in the rock.

1. Cathedral of Virgin Mary in Atskuri
2. Atskuri Fortress
3. General View of Atskuri Fortress from the Church
4. View at River Mtkvari from Atskuri Fortress

78 AKHALTSIKHE

Akhaltsikhe is one of the oldest towns of Georgia (old name – Lomsia). It is located in 230 km from Tbilisi, in the Akhaltsikhe plain, on both banks of river Potskhovi. In historical sources it is mentioned from XII century. In XIII-XIV centuries it is a political center of Samtskhe-Saatabago. In 1629-1828 it became part of the Ottoman empire as a capital of Akhaltsikhe vilayet and a seat of Pasha. It used to be the most important center of prisoner slave trade. Historical part of the town of Akhaltsikhe was built on the rocky mount on the left bank of river Potskhovistskali. It is called Rabat that means a settlment of merchants and artisans in the medieval town. On the territory of Rabat is located the fortress of Sargis Jakeli, church of St. Marina, palace of Pashas of Akhaltsikhe, Ottoman mosque (1752), Karavan-sarai, baths. On the territory of Rabat in Akhaltsikhe today operates local history museum.

1. Rabat Mosque in Akhaltsikhe
2. Karavan-sarai
3. Mosque (interior)
4. Armed Stella from Rabat museum (XII c.)
5. Stone Stella with Image of Coat of Arms, Samtskhe Principality
6. Exibits of Akhaltsikhe Museum

79 VANI CAVES

Vani Caves monastery complex carved in the rock (VIII-XVI cc.) is located in Javakheti, 27 km from Aspindza, on the right bank of river Mtkvari. In the center of the monastery stands church of St. George which was carved from the stone along with the main part of caves and cells in IX-XI cc. In 1089 an earthquake seriously damaged Vani Caves. Its patron Ichkit Gurgenisdze started restoration of the monastery in 1186-1191, he restored church of St. George and family anteroom adjacent to it, and emphasized a donator inscription at both entrances. In 1204 Anton Mtsignobartukhutsesi-Chkondideli revived a limestone barrier to the monastery. In 1204-1283 the monastery was supervised by the sovereigns of Javakheti – the Tmogveli. They established Rules for the monastery 'Vani Cave Providence' (1204-1234), built anteroom, belfry of the church of St. George and a hall church (1265-1283). In 1283 earthquake again destroyed Vani Caves. In 1551 and in 1576 the monastery underwent assaults of the Persians and the Ottomans. After that the monastery ceased its operation.

Vani Caves include 200 caves carved in the rock (cells, anterooms, burial site, asylum, support stock rooms, communication caves and 6 churches) which are arranged in 16 floors. Water pool and remnants of 3 tracks of running water are extant. Archeological excavations have discovered 8 wine cellars, sats-nakheli (grapes pressing tub) carved in the rock, ceramic shop. Scholars believe that construction and architectural experience of Vani Caves had prepared conditions for creation of Vardzia complex carved in the rock.

On the last floor of Vani Caves, on the walls of a built-in church there are extant fresco painting of XII-XIII centuries and inscriptions of historical content, including those performed by nuns (Gulkan, Ana Rcheulishvili, Tumian Gojishvili...) using Mkhedruli script (XV c.). In inscriptions they make complaints of their misfortune. Nuns scribed on the wall also 2 lines from Vepkhistkaosani (Knight in the Tiger's Skin): a part of a letter written by Nestan-Darejan to Tariel (1300; 1301) as well as pleasant lyrical poems.

1. Vani Caves (Cells of Left Slopes)
2. Upper Church Carved in the Rock
3. Vani Caves (Cells of Right Slopes)
4. Inscriptions of Nuns at Vani Caves

80 VARDZIA

Monastery complex carved in the rock (1156-1203) stands in Javakheti, 30 km from Aspindza, on the left bank of river Mtkvari. Ioane Shavteli worked in Vardzia, extant are his ,Littanies of Vardzia the Virgin Mary'. Preacher of the Vardzia monastery was simultaneously a high profile servant at the Royal Court – Satsolis Mtsignobari and was in charge of operation of monasteries.

In 1551 during invasion of the Shah of Iran, Tahmasp I, the Icon of the Virgin Mary, gold and metal gates and much jewelry were stolen from Vardzia. After invasion of the Ottomans, from 1578 Vardzia became deserted. In 1938 Vardzia received a status of a sanctuary museum. In the beginning of XXI century monastery activity was restored at Vardzia.

Vardzia monastery has the width of 0,5 km and is arranged on 13 floors. It consists of 2 parts: rock village of Ananauri (X-XI cc.), monastery itself built in 5 stages: on the first stage, during the reign of Giorgi III (1156-1184), first cells and a church were carved. On the second stage, during the reign of Queen Tamar (1184-1185), in the center of the monastery was carved a hall church of Assumption of Virgin Mary with stoa. At the expense of Kartli sovereign, Rati Surameli, the church was painted by an artist Giorgi. On the third stage (1185-1203), construction of stockrooms and cells, fortification and irrigation facilities was over. Earthquake in 1283 was followed by IV stage of the construction of monastery carried out by the head of Samtskhe, Beka Jakeli (1285-1306). He masterminded construction of a two-story ornamented bell tower. On the V stage (middle of XIV century), under Ivane Atabaghi's auspices, was carved a big refectory. Overall, Vardzia consists of 420 utility rooms. Among them are 25 wine cellars with 185 barrels. There are 2, 3, 4-room living cells consisting of a gate, a room and a stockroom. There are wide cavities carved in the walls of rooms – just to lie, and small niches – for utencils, books and earthen saucer. Totally there are 12 chapels in the monastery.

The best preserved at the monastery is eastern part – 242 carved rooms (including a hall of 8 m x 5,6 m, assembly hall, Tamar's room, feast room). In the western part of the monastery is a refectory, in central part – asylum rooms. Tunnels were supplied from natural spring existing in the depth behind the main church (with the help of 3,5 km running water system).

Vardzia is rich with fresco paintings. In the XII century church of Assumption of Virgin Mary there are images of donators: Giorgi III, Queen Tamar, Rati Surameli. There are also scenes from the New Testament. Painting of Ananauri church belongs to XVI century.

1. **Right Part of Vardzia (View from the Belfry)**
2. **Portraits of Vardzia Donators: Queen Tamar, Giorgi III**
3. **Tunnel Connecting Cells**
4. **Vardzia (General view)**
5. **Fresco Painting of the Church of Assumption of Virgin Mary**

81 FORTRESS OF KHERTVISI AND TSUNDA

Khertvisi is a medieval fortress on the border of Samtskhe and Javakheti, it stands on the strategically important venue, at the confluence of rivers Paravani and Mtkvari, on the high rocky mountain. Its name is related to the geographic location of the fortress. Khertvisi fortress comes across in historical sources from XI century. In 1578-1829 Khertvisi fortress was the seat of Ottoman garrison and administrative center. There are traces of a lot of renovations (Georgian, Russian, Ottoman) conducted at the fortress. Khertvisi fortress is noted with big space and a number of utility rooms. It has an unaccessible citadel, court church. The fortress was supplied with water through a tunnel constructed from south-west.

Tsunda was the old political and religious center of Javakheti. Nowadays this place is called the village of Nakalakevi (old city). It is located on the right bank of river Mtkvari. As the historical sources report, the city was founded by Etnarkh Javakhos. The founder of the Kingdom of Kartli, king Parnavaz (IV-III cc. BC) turned Tsunda into a center of the Principality. It was placed on the important trade and military routes. Church of Tsunda was erected on the small rock and it is a hall church constructed in XII-XIII centuries with quadrangular stone. The church is richly ornamented. On the western gate there is an inscription in Asomtavruli. An anteroom with ornamented columns is attached to the south. The architectural idea of the church was implemented originally. One can enter the internal courtyard encircled by the fence only through the church.

1. Khertvisi Fortress (General view)
2. Tsunda (View from the South)
3. Tsunda (View from the West)
4. Donator Inscription on the Tsunda Church

82 SAPARA AND ZARZMA

Sapara – a medieval Georgian monastery and one of the residences and bureal sites of the rulers of Samtskhe, the Jakeli family - is located in 12 km to the south-east from the town of Akhaltsikhe. The oldest construction of the complex – church of Assumption dates from X century, and the main part (main dome church of St. Saba, belfry and palace) were constructed on the edge of XIII-XIV cc., during the rule of the sovereign of Samtskhe, Beka Jakeli (1285-1309).

On the southern wall of the church of St. Saba are depicted donators of the monastery – family portraits of Jakeli: Sargis I (1266-1285) who was ordained as a priest under the name of Saba, his son Beka I – with a model of a church, Beka's children Sargis II (1309-1334) and Kvarkvare (1334-1360). To the west of the cathedral, at the top of an anteroom window, there is an inscription of its builder Parezasdze. Cathedral both in the interior and from outside is adorned with various decor and ornaments. Bell tower located to the west of the main cathedral is the family cemetery of the Msakhurtukhutsesi (Chief minister) of the Jakeli family, Lasurisdze. There are ruins of the old fortress overlooking the monastery from western side. During domination of the Ottomans, in XVI century, monks left the monastery. The monastery life was renewed in Sapara in XIX century.

The Zarzma monk monastery is located in the historical Samtskhe, 12 km from the town of Adigeni. It consists of dome church, belfry and one-nave chapel. The monastery first was allegedly founded by the Klarjeti monk, Serapion (his life is described in the hagiographic treatise by Basil Zarzmeli Life of Serapion Zarzmeli) in IX century. A local noble, Giorgi Chorchaneli, helped him in his endeavor to build a monastery and had even sacrificed villages for the newly-founded monastery. The church of Serapion's time which does not exist any more was built by architect Garbaneli.

The current complex of Zarzma was built in the beginning of XIV century by the sovereign of Samtskhe,

Beka Jakeli (1285-1309). The oldest historical remains of the monastery are a built-in inscription of X century on the entrance arch (tells about march of king David III Kurapalat to Barda Skliaros) which was removed from the previous construction.

Zarzma is adorned with numerous ornaments. It is rich with fresco painting. There are portraits of secular church wardens beside religious scenes. On the southern wall there are family portraits of rulers of Samtskhe – the Jakeli family (Sargis I – 1266-1285); Beka I – 1285-1309; Sargis II – 1309-1334; Kvarkvare – 1334-1360). On the Northern wall there is XVI century painting.

Belfry of Zarzma is one of the biggest belfries in Georgia. On the I floor of the belfry some Khurtsidze opened a church of John the Baptist in XVI century. At the beginning of the XX century Georgian Exarchate of the Russian church made a restoration work of Zarzma. The painted part and iconostasis were changed during the works.

1. Monastery of Sapara (View from the South)
2. Zarzma (View from the West)
3. Donator Portraits of Samtskhe Sovereigns: Sargis I, Beka and Sargis II Jakeli

AJARA

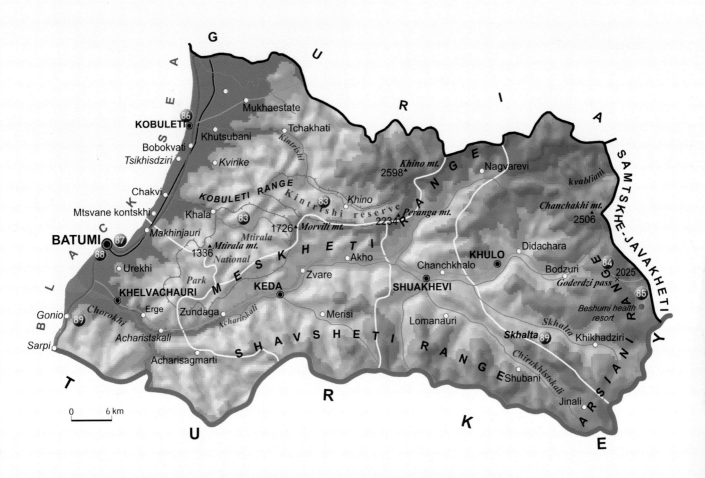

83. Kintrishi and Mtirala Protected Territories

84. Goderdzi Petrified Flora

85. Beshumi

86. Resort of Kobuleti

87. Batumi Botanical Garden (Green Cape)

88. Batumi

89. Gonio-Aphsaro and Skhalta

83 KINTRISHI AND MTIRALA PROTECTED TERRITORIES

Kintrishi and Mtirala protected territories are located on the territory of Ajara, 320-340 km from Tbilisi, on the Western slopes of Ajara-Imereti mountain range, in the gorge of river Kintrishi and in the vicinity of the town of Kobuleti. It includes two parts – Kintrishi sanctuary and Mtirala national park. Kintrishi sanctuary was founded in 1959 and Mtirala national park - nearly half a century later, in 2006.

Protected territories stretch on the slopes lying perpendicular to the wind masses blown from Black sea. Here, in the vicinity of Mtirala mountain, precipitation exceeds 4 thousand mm that is the highest parameter not only in the Caucasus but also in Europe. Proximity of Black sea and big volume of precipitation determine formation of moist subtropical climate and forceful Kolkheti forests.

Mountain relief of protected territories includes several hypsometric stages and has an outstanding relative height that determines vertical belt and, accordingly, natural variety.

Protected territories are known for unheard of diversity of Kolkheti vegetation. By occupied space in forests predominant are beech, chestnut and hornbeam groves. From the relicts it is worth mentioning pontine oak (Quercus pontica), birch tree (Betula medwedewii), rhododendron (Rhododendron ungernii), yew, ruscus (Ruscus ponticus), Caucasian persimmon (Diospyros lotus), sweet chestnut (Castanea sativa), et al. In the forests powerful underbushes are dispersed where several species of liana, Kolkheti misletow, holly and cherry laurel dominate.

The fauna of perotected territories is rich with birds, mammals, fish, reptiles, et al. From predators there are such species as bear, wolf, lynx, fox, small eagle, hawk, falcon, horned owl, scops-owl, owl, et al.

Protected territories are located near Georgia's biggest sea and spa tourism centers (Kvariati, Batumi, Chakvi, Kobuleti). Region is rich with historic and archeological monuments. Among them are ancient Gonio (Apsarunt) Fortress and ruins, many medieval churches, mosques and fortresses.

Goderdzi petrified flora is in the vicinity of Gorerdzi mountain pass (2025 meters above the sea level). It is located in the south-western part of Georgia, on the mountain range of Arsiani meridian direction.

Geological history of the range relates to underwater volcano activity thanks to which it is arranged in volcanic rocks known under the name of Goderdzi Waters. In its eastern part were discovered Tertiary period fragments of petrified flora that is a world-important unique natural attraction.

Petrified flora originated several million years ago as a result of volcano activity. Volcanic ashes and lava covered powerful tropical forest where tens of species of plants were represented. The fate of tropical forest is compared with that of Pompeii. Remnants of under-Tertiary period plants (palm, magnolia, laurel, birch, hornbeam, beech-likes and other) are represented here in the form of petrified and half-petrified trees and traces of leaves.

Goderdzi petrified flora turned out to be the best specimen of paleo-geography and evolution of plants. With its help it was established that in that era, on the territory of the Caucasus, climate and vegetation that were typical for the humid tropical belt, dominated in the area. There were both ever-green and leafy species, underbushes and lianas, plural filices and plural herbs scattered in the forests. Nowadays such forests are dispersed in Japan, Australia and South America.

85 BESHUMI

Beshumi is a mountain resort which is located on the eastern knees of Arsiani mountain range, 1900 meters above the sea level. Here is a mixture of windy masses blowing from Black sea, high-mountain meadows and medium-size dark coniferous forests. Within the borders of a resort there are several mineral water springs of medicinal value actively used for curing alimentary tract.

Beshumi's importance as a resort is linked to comfortable climate, pure and sound air. Holiday season continues several months – from June to

September. Air is very effective for treatment of respiratory tracts and chronic diseases of children.

In the environs of Beshumi tourist infrastructure is swiftly developing. This is true especially for skiing and mountain climbing. Every year powerful, dry and long-standing snow blanket shapes up here which along with the smooth forms of relief is a good precondition for paving routes for skiing.

86 RESORT OF KOBULETI

Resort of Kobuleti is situated in the Black sea belt, in the extreme south-western point of Kolkheti lowland. Its population is up to 20 thousand people. In the holiday season the town has numerous visitors.

Resort is known for its comfortable climate and developped tourist infrastructure. The average temperature in January is more than +5⁰C, and in July - +22⁰-25⁰C. The volume of precipitation attains 2000 mm compensated by considerable days without precipitation during holiday season. The temperature of the sea water at the same season is +23-+24⁰C that increases recreational importance of the resort.

Kobuleti's petty-fraction sea beach is stretched on 10 km of the sea coastline. Between the beach and settlement area there is a 3-4 meter high and several tens of meters wide strip of coast dunes where impressive pine groves are cultivated. Pine grove creates special micro-climate which is unmatched medicinal cure for cardio-vascular system and lung diseases.

Near Kobuleti are situated Kolkheti humid protected territories, Kintrishi sanctuary and Mtirala national park that increases its recreational function.

Batumi botanical garden, or Green Cape is situated on the Black sea coast, to the north from the city and extends over 111 hectares. The cultivation of the botanical garden was launched back in 1889 by a famous decorator and chief gardener of Batumi, D'Alphonse. From southern France he imported a big number of plant cultures. From 1912 Professor A. Krasnov created a project for development of a garden. He invited Yason Gordeziani for the position of a chief gardener under leadership of whom Japanese, Chinese, Mexican, Australian, Chilean, New Zealand, American and European divisions were developped. Batumi botanical garden is a member of the International Union for Conservation of Nature and Natural Resources (IUCN).

There are 3 exotic plant plots, a sanctuary of Kolkheti forest and 9 florist divisions created on the principle of geography of landscape. Botanical garden is one of the outstanding in the world by its space, species diversity and age.

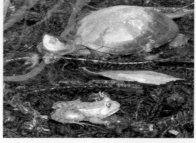

88 BATUMI

The city of Batumi is located in Western Georgia, on the coastline of Black sea, on the cape of Batumi, on the coast of Batumi gulf and adjacent hillocks. Batumi is an administrative, economic, cultural and educational center of Autonomous Republic of Ajara. Its favorable geographic location became a precondition of maritime transit development. Today it is considered to be a maritime gate of Georgia.

Batumi's climate is humid subtropical. It is the warmest place in Georgia. The average temperature in January is +7⁰C. Summer is relatively cool (+22-+24⁰C) that increases the city's importance as a resort area. Snow cover is available only in certain years for several days. The Western knees of the Ajara-Imereti mountain range near Batumi are covered with Kolkheti polydominant forests, and all this overall creates inimitable sceneries. In recent years the number of Batumi recreational visitors is constantly on the rise.

Batumi was a settlement in as early as Antique era (it was first mentioned by Aristotle under the name of Athus) and had trade relationships with ancient Greek cities. In II century a Roman garrison was stationed here. In Middle Ages, on the site of today's Batumi existed a village-like settlement surrounding The Fortress of Tamar. In XV-XVI centuries Batumi was governed by Guria sovereigns, and in XVII-XIX centuries it was a part of the Ottoman empire. In

1878 according to the Berlin treaty Batumi was handed over to the Russian empire; until 1886 it enjoyed porto-franko status which became a reason of Batumi's swift development. That time it was a leading city in the Caucasus, a port, a corridor for transit of oil from Baku to Europe and a district administrative center. From 1919 Batumi became the center of the Georgian Muslim autonomy within the Democratic Republic of Georgia, and from 1921 it is a center of Ajara Autonomy in Georgia.

European style of buildings is typical for Batumi chatecterized by convergence of modern and XIX century architecture. There are many historical and architectural attractions in Batumi: cathedral of the Virgin Mary (former Catholic cathedral in 1898-2902 which was built under sponsorship of brothers Zubalashvili who were doing their business in Baku. In Soviet era the Bolsheviks shut down the church. In 1989 the Orthodox congregation of the church restarted its operation); Batumi Boulevard (in 1881 a famous gardener Ressler and after him D'Alphonse and Yason Gordeziani step-by-step created a coastline park. In 1934 was erected a symbol of the park – a Collonnade. Until 2004 the length of the Boulvarde was 2 km. Today its length is raised up to 15 km); building of Shota Rustaveli University (built in 1903 as a gymnasium. Several years ago was rehabilitated); hotel Intourist Palace (a specimen of Stalin architecture, was built near coastline park in 1939 on design of Professor Shchusev); Batumi Ilia Chavchavadze State Theater (was built in 1952 on design of architect Teplitski); 6 May Park and Lake Nurigheli (constructed in 1881. In recent years was fundamentally refurbished: roads and paths were made, park benches put up, new attractions installed, illumination sorted out, dolphinarium, aquarium and zoo corner restored); Jewish sinagogue (was built by Semeon Vulkovicz in 1904); a mosque Orta Jame (was built in 1886 with financing of Aslan-beg Khimshiashvili).

1. Dountown Batumi. Europe Square
2. Renovated Boulevard of Batumi
3. Batumi Cathedral of the Virgin Mary

89 GONIO—APHSAROS AND SKHALTA

The fortress belonging to the Antique and Middle-Age era is situated 12 km south of the city of Batumi, on the left bank of river Chorokhi. The fortress of Gonio-Apsarosi had a unque strategic importance: it defended entrances to the Chorokhi and Ajaristskali gorges which connected internal regions of south-west Georgia with the Black sea coast. Thanks to this location the fortress of Gonio was turned into one of the backbone citadels of first Rome and later Byzantine Empires in the area of Black sea. First reference of the fortress of Gonio in the historical sources under the name of Apsarunt belongs to author Plinius Secundus (Pliny the Elder) (I c.). The Apsarunt fortress used to be a well reinforced and conveniently fortified town where 5 Roman cohorts (3 000 warriors) had a station. Due to strategic location, it always was a focal point for Rome, Byzantine and Genoa republics. In 1547-1878 it fell under control of the Ottoman empire.

From XII century on the fortress is referred to as the Gonio fortress. It is a stone-made big rectangle (195m x 245m). The fence is reinforced with 18 towers. Each side has one gate. There are several construction layers on the fortress (III-IV cc., VI-VII cc., XVI c.). Today the fortress is renovated and is the biggest fortified facility in the whole of Georgia.

As the reference goes, this is the place where king Ayeti laid to rest his son, Aphsaros, killed by escaped Jason who dismembered the corpse and scattered its parts over the sea. As the legend goes, one of the prophets of Christ – Matata is also buried in Gonio.

The center of Skhalta Eparchy – the church of Skhalta is located in Upper Ajara, in Khulo region. It was built in XIII century. It is built on the slope, has no dome and is covered by a gable roof. Interior of the church and outer casing are made with cut stone. The eastern façade is decorated with ornamented crosses. The church of Skhalta is a formidable monument in southern Georgia.

1. Fence of Gonio Fortress
2. Gonio Fortress
3. Skhalta (View from East)
4. Skhalta (View from South-West)

ABKHAZIA
OCCUPIED TERRITORY

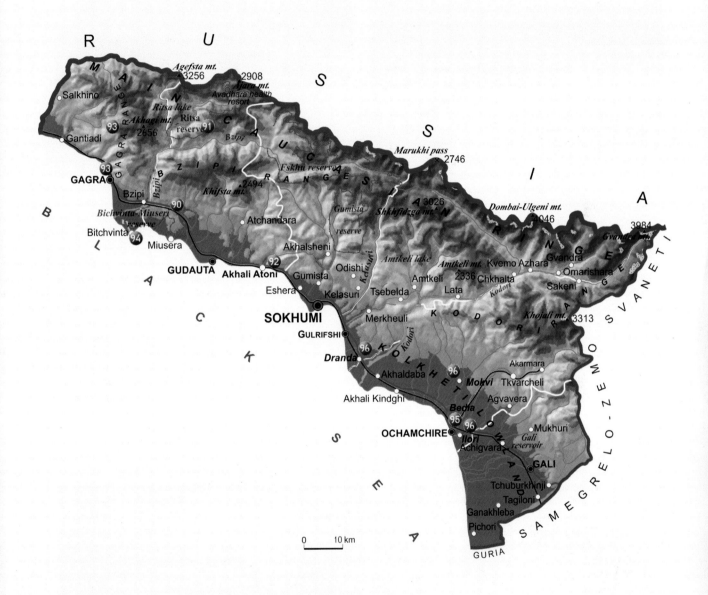

90. Bichvinta-Musera Sanctuary

91. Ritsa Protected Territories

92. Cave of Akhali Atoni (Iveria)

93. Resort of Gagra and Gagra Mountain Range

94. Bichvinta and Besleti Bridge

95. Bedia Cathedral

96. Mokvi, Ilori and Dranda

90 BICHVINTA—MUSERA SANCTUARY

Buchvinta-Musera sanctuary is located in the north-western part of Georgia, in Abkhazia, in the Black sea belt, between Bichvinta cape and Musera (Kovaluk) upland. It was set up in 1966 aiming at protection of the last residue of Crimea-Caucasus Tertiary period – relict pine of Bichvinta and polydominant Colchis forest. The area of the sanctuary is 3.7 sq. km where more than 100 ha are covered by relict pine-tree groves.

Bichvinta relict pine-tree groves are dispersed on the cape of Bichvinta, in the dune strip of Black sea. The height of the cape is 1,5-3 m. The name of the cape is linked to the Greek name of pine-tree. There are several thousand pine-tree species here having the height of 40 meters and age of 130 years. The pine groves are under protection from 1885.

Sanctuary is located on the brink of sub-tropical and moderate belts. The average temperature in January is +6°C, and in August - +22-+23°C. The climate is humid subtropical, however by the volume of precipitation (1400 mm) and its spread (maximum in winter and minimum in summer) it is similar to that of Mediterranean. The temperature of sea water in January is +8,5°C that is rather high indicator for these latitudes.

Many plant species of Buchvinta-Musera sanctuary are listed in the Red Book. The special interest is attracted by relict pine-tree of Bichvinta groves which are unique for recreational and health care purposes.

There are also such endemic species as Colchis mistletoe, wingnuts (Pterocarya pterocarpa), Colchis ivy (Hedera colchica), Caucasian linden (Tilia caucasica), Georgian and Hartwiss oak (Quercus hartwissiana), chestnut, et al.

The environs of the sanctuary are rich with historical and archeological monuments. This territory in Antique times was handled and described by the Greeks. Many artefacts of Bronze Age, Antique era and early Middle Ages were discovered here. Within the resort of Bichvinta are the ruins of V century three-nave basilica and X century cross-dome cathedral.

91 RITSA PROTECTED TERRITORIES

Ritsa protected territories (nowadays having the status of national park) is located in the extreme south-west of Georgia, in Abkhazia, on the southern slope of Kavkasioni, in the eastern mountain range of Gagra, in the catchment area of river Bzipi, basically around the lake of Ritsa. Today its area attains 400 sq. km. The Ritsa sanctuary was set up in 1930.

The protected territory hypsometrically is spread on 3 kilometers that is the cause of its natural diversity. The distribution of height is characteristic both for climate and soil, vegetation and landscapes.

The Ritsa unique lake is within the frames of protected territories and is of landslide origin. Thanks to big depth (101 m), cold-water inflows and high station (900 meters above the sea level), in summer its water temperature attains only $+20^{\circ}$C.

Favorable natural conditions determine variety of life in the sanctuary. Especially rich is its flora where up to 1500 species are represented. Caucasian fir-tree (Abies nordmanniana) stands out in terms of occupied space, creates around lake Ritsa incomparable scenery and gives water green hue. From other species beech and oak groves should be noted in terms of occupied territory. In the underbush dominates Colchis misletoe covering hundreds of hectares.

Protected territories are rich with birds, fish, mammals, rodents, amphibians, et al. Here made its habitat the smallest predator weasel (Mustela nivalis) and the biggest one - bear (Ursus arctos).

Protected territories area is rich with archeological and historic monuments. Here was discovered a human settlement dating to Palaeolithic era, are extant ruins of fortress towns and early medieval churches, etc.

Lake Ritsa is situated in Abkhazia, in the gorge of river Iupshara, 884 meters above the sea level. It is distinguished with depth and unmatched beauty in Georgia and also in the whole Caucasus. It should be emphasized that the lake's bed is constantly expanding because of accumulation of suspended materials proved by research conducted in the course of last century. According to the findings, it became evident that every year it gains 32 sm. The lake originated 250-300 years ago resulting congestion of river Lashipse by a rockslide. Today 6 rivers flow into it, and only one – Iupshara flows out. In spring the water level increases by several meters related to intensive melting of snow. Lake Ritsa is the most important natural drawcard and recreational region of Abkhazia.

92 CAVE OF AKHALI ATONI (IVERIA)

Cave of Akhali Atoni is located in Abkhazia, in the Black sea coast strip, in the lower part of Bzipi mountain range. Its entrance is on 220 meters above the sea level. It was discovered in 1961 but for tourism purposes it has been operating from 1975.

Cave of Akhali Atoni is one of the exceptional karstifications in the world. It consists of several interconnected halls with general space of 50 thousand sq.m and volume of 1,5 million cubic meters. The interior within the cave is decorated with various forms made of calcite that create exclusive show.

Cave of Akhali Atoni consists both from vertical (overall depth 183 m) and horizontal (overall length 3285 m) parts. There are five big halls there of which by geometrical characteristics the Hall of Georgian Speleologists stands out. It is the biggest in Europe.

Temperature in the cave is characterized by insignificant circulation and swings (2.5^0C – in summer). There are three lakes there which get their feed from both vertical and horizontal flows. Underground fauna is especially rich represented there with worms, mollusca, crawfish, spider, insects and bats.

Cave of Akhali Atoni is a formidable spot for tourism. In particular years millions of visitors travelled from various countries of the world to see it.

93 RESORT OF GAGRA AND GAGRA MOUNTAIN RANGE

Resort of Gagra is located in Western Georgia, in Abkhazia, on the Black sea coast, on the south-western slope of the Gagra mountrain range. Humans here settled several thousand years ago, however the function of a resort town Gagra obtained only in the beginning of XX century. The climate of Gagra and temperature of Black sea water on holiday season (+24-+26^{0}C) are overly comfortable. The temperature swings of air runs to 17^{0}C and aridity index is 1,4. Humid wind blowing from the sea easily passes through the mountain range standing in parallel to its direction. Sea and curative climatic resort of Gagra gains special effectiveness from mineral waters and mountain slopes reaching the coastline and guised in Colchis forests.

The mountain range of Gagra is a branch of Western Kavkasioni. It is a watershed of rivers Psou and Bzipi. Mount Agepsda (3257 m) which is the highest crest of the range is simultaneously the most extreme north-western point of Georgia.

Gagra range developed glaciers in Quaternary period evidenced by cirques, gates and gorges. On

some small fragments of the range there are modern glaciers, too.

Limestone structure of Gagra range is precondition of karst form development of relief which come into sight as karst craters and abysses, the deepest in Europe. In the karst crevasses big volume of waters move on – these waters find their ultimate point in river gorges, coastline and even seabed. One of them represented by river Reprua flows directly to the coast of the sea. Its length from its source to confluence point is 20 meters due to which river Reprua is the shortest in the world.

Mountain range stuck to the coast of the sea, visible vertical position, moderate precipitation, deciduous Colchis forests and duration of snow blanket in sub-Alpine zone make scenery of the resort of Gagra unmatched. In the vicinity of the resoirt stands crest of Mamzishkha on some segment of which snow cover lasts until the end of July. Such 'mixture' of sea, sun and snow in summer months which is very rare in the world is a wonderful precondition of development of sea and mountain tourism.

94 BICHVINTA AND BESLETI BRIDGE

Bichvinta is located on the territory of Abkhazia currently occupied by Russia, 80 km from Sokhumi and 22 km from Gagra. The township type settlement here existed in Antique era. The word Bichvinta is a translation of a Greek name Pitiunt (Pitious in ancient Greek means 'Pine-tree').

Bronze hatchets and ceramics treasure discovered on Bichvinta cape prove that on the edge of II-I millennia there were ancient Colchis settlements there. Archeologists exposed ceramics covered with red varnish, numismatic materials (coins of Roman emperors and Trapesunt town coins), artefacts with Greek and Latin inscriptions.

Bichvinta first was mentioned in the work of Greek geographer Strabo (I c. BC) titled the Great Pitiunt. In II-III cc. here was a station of Roman garrison which defended the Empire from invasions of northern nomadic tribes. Archeological excavations within the fortress of Bichvinta have discovered a bath, wine cellar, ruins of goldsmith and ceramic shops, sewerage system. Here also stands a three-nave richly decorated basilica of IV century with its mosaic floor preserved up to present day.

Bichvinta is the oldest center of Christianity in the Caucasus. In IV century there was an Episcopal cathedra while Bishop Stratophilos was a participant in the I Ecumenical Council of the Church (325). In IX-XVI centuries Bichvinta was a seat of a Primate of West Georgia Church – Catholicos. In the center of Bichvinta stands a big cross-dome cathedral (X c.). After moving of the residence of Abkhazia Episcopacy to Gelati (in 50-ies of the XVI century) Bichvinta monastery became deserted. In XIX century its walls were whitened but extant are fragments of XVI century mural painting. According to legend here was laid to rest St. John Chrysostom, also St. Andrew the First-called and Simon the Kananites whose symbolic graves are lined-up within the building.

On the river Besleti near the city of Sokhumi there is an extant arch bridge of 13 m x 4,7 m length and 6 m height. On the face stones of the arch there is a carved Georgian inscription in Asomtavruli. In the Middle Age Georgia the Royal administration aiming at facilitation of trade built across rivers bridges which were used by caravans for hauling cargoes across rivers. Such bridges were built of limestone tiles joined together with lime mortar. It is decorated with cut blocks of stone. The arch of the bridge is supported by an abutment installed on both river banks. On the elevated arch earthfills are made on both sides. Such arch bridges are often called Bridges of Queen Tamar. One- and two-span bridges are preserved in especially big numbers in southern Georgia, to wit Ajara. The biggest part of arch stone bridges are preserved at present on rivers Ajaristskali, Machakhela and Kintrishi. There are up to ten such bridges in Ajara: arch bridges of Purtio, Tskhemlari, Makhuntseti, Dandalo, Tskhemovani, Kobalauri and others. There are many extant buttresses of arch bridges also outside of the confines of Georgia – on the territories of Shavshet-Imerkhevi and Lazika.

1. Bichvinta Cathedral (View from South-East)
2. Mozaic of Bichvinta Cathedral
3. Besleti Bridge

95 BEDIA CATHEDRAL

Bedia monastery complex is situated on the territory of Abkhazia currently occupied by Russia, 25 km from the town of Ochamchire, in the center of the hamlet of Bedia.

According to the historical data, the main cathedral of the Virgin Mary was built roughly in 999 by the first king of the united Georgia, Bagrat III Bagrationi (978-1014), who turned it into a seat of Episcopacy. Bagrat III himself and his mother, queen Gurandukht are buried exactly in the Bedia monastery. In the interior of the cathedral three layers of fresco painting have been preserved which are dated to X-XI, XIII-XIV and XVI-XVII centuries. In the eastern part of southern wall among others there are images of cathedral donator – Bagrat III with a model of cathedral in his hand, and representatives of Dadiany family. Bedia Episcopacy was one of the most important religious and cultural and educational centers in Middle Ages.

To the west of the cathedral is located a two-story palace of Bedia metropolitans (was built by Bedia Metropolitan Anton Zhuanisdze), and in front of the northern entrance stands a belfry (XIV c.). Bedia monastery was renovated in XIII-XIV centuries.

Bedia monastery is related to Gold Chalice (999) – a church vessel made of pure gold. Its height is 12,5 sm, diameter – 14 sm, the support leg of the vessel is lost. The Chalice's outer surface is devided on 12 arches. Under every arch there is an image of a saint. On the opposite arches there are images of Jesus Christ and the Virgin Mary with a child. On the upper part of the Chalice is a one-line Asomtavruli inscription from which it is clear that this Chalice was made on order of Bagrat III and his mother, queen Gurandukht, and then bestowed to Bedia monastery. The Badia Chalice is under custody of the Georgian State Museum of Culture.

1. Bedia Cathedral
2. Bagrat III (Fresco of Bedia Cathedral)
3. Bedia Chalice

96 MOKVI, ILORI AND DRANDA

Mokvi is situated on the bank of river Mokvistskali, 17 km from Ochamchire, on the territory of Abkhazia currently occupied by Russia. The X century cathedral was built by king of the Abkhaz, Leon III. Cathedral is a specimen of confluence of theree-nave basilica and dome church. Chapels are placed in the side naves. Cathedral had a rich book depository. Among the books stand out Mokvi Gospels (1301) which are now in custody of the Center of Georgian Manuscripts.

Dranda Episcopacy cathedral is located in 18 km from Sokhumi, to the south-east, on the right bank of river Kodori, on the elevated plateau, in the hamlet of Dranda, on the territory of Abkhazia currently occupied by Russia. Dranda cathedral is considered to be one of the variants of Mtskheta Jvari along with Byzantine elements and is dated to VII-VIII centuries. Cathedral was damaged many times during the reign of the Turks (XVII-XVIII cc.) and frescoes of XIII-XIV centuries were erazed. In 1880-83 Dranda cathedral was renovated and monk monastery was established which existed until 1921. In 1978 repair and rehabilitation works were carried on in Dranda aiming at restoration of original face of the monument.

Ilori church of St. George is the most important house of worship in Western Georgia. It is located in 3 km from Ochamchire, on the territory of Abkhazia currrently occupied by Russia. The monument of the I quarter of XI century is a one-nave building completed with apse and annexes in the north, south and west. On the eastern facade there are extant inscriptions. In Middle Ages it was part of the Odishi principality. In XVII century Levan II Dadiani refurbished it. In 1736 was burned down by the Turks. In the 40-ies of XIX century was fundamentally renovated. Near cathedral there are ruins of a fortress of early feudal era.

St. George festivities used to be held in Ilori. The clergy of Odishi conducted a ritual. As sacrificial offering were used white-patch bulls which were picked by St. George himself and its meat was distributed to worshippers. Part of meat was kept as a defender from evil and sinister disease. In ancient era instead of a bull sacrificial animal was deer which as reported went to Cathedral himself.

1. Mokvi Cathedral
2. Mokvi Gospel
3. Church of St. George in Ilori
4. Dranda Episcopacy Cathedral

NATURAL
DRAWCARDS

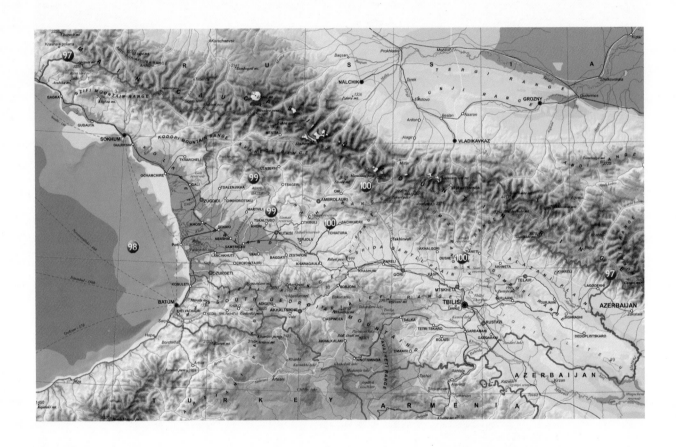

97. Kavkasioni

98. Black sea

99. Limestone Massifs

100. Geomorphological Rocks

Kavkasioni is a new mountain system of sublatitude direction which stretches on 1100 km from Black sea to Caspian sea. Its highest peak from the sea level - 5642 meters on Mount Elbrus – is registered in Kabardino-Balkaria.

Kavkasioni is one of the important geographic objects in Europe due to which many piculiarities of geographic developments in the Caucasus took place. It has also a function of fundamental barrier (both natural and political). It separates from each other: moderate and subtropical belts, rivers of Azov, Black and Caspian sea basins; northern and southern Caucasus; Russia, Georgia and Azerbaijan.

The highest part of Central Kavkasioni is structured from oldest, 600 million-year granites and crystal tiles. In its western and eastern parts geological structure becomes simpler that is the indicator of the development of mountain range.

Along with decrease of height the age of buttress rocks goes down. In middle mountains we come across 200-130 million year mountains (Jurasic era) and 130-70 million-year mountains (limestone), in lowland and foothills – 70-30 million year (paleogenic) rocks.

Process of mountain-building in Kavkasioni continues. High-swing earthquakes often happen here that proves

intensity of modern mountain-building. It is established that Kavkasioni is gaining in height 10 mm per year which is a rather high indicator.

Kavkasioni crests are covered with permanent glaciers and snow. There are up to 800 glaciers with general space of 550 sq. km. By this indicator Kavkasioni is rather close to Western Alps, therefore, French and Georgian glaciers occupy roughly the same space.

Kavkasioni is a mountain system distinguished with its effective landscapes, biological and ethnic diversity. There are several historical and geographic provinces remained here which are chatacterized with unique cultural and economic traditions. Here is located also the hamlet of Ushguli which is the highest human settlement in Europe.

98 BLACK SEA

Black sea borders Georgia in the west. It has geo-political, resource bringing, climate shaping, transit and recreational importance. It is a gate to world ocean for the Georgians. Within the country the total length of the sea border line (3400 km) is represented with only 9% share.

At first the Greeks called Black sea Pontos Axeinos ('inhospitable sea'), later (from AD) - Euxeinos Pontos ('hospitable sea'). From XV century the Ottoman Turks called it Kara Denizi, or Black sea.

Geological history of the development of Black sea is complex and interesting. Eight million years ago it used to be a part of Pontos sea (together with Caspian sea). One million years ago Pontos sea was divided in two parts. After that Black sea merged and parted several times with saline Mediterranean sea. Each merger caused destruction of fresh water fauna in Black sea.

Within the coastline of Georgia Black sea is the most comfortable. Salination of water does not exceed 0.2-0.3% that is several times lower than this indicator in its central and southern parts. Transparency of water is not too high (6-8 m), however its summer temperature (+24-+26⁰C) is the most appropriate from recreational and curative standpoints. Likewise, also comfortable is speed of coast current excelling 1 km/h.

The world of see plants and animals is diverse. It is noted for its variety of plankton and wildlife species. More than 200 species of fish made their habitat here of which about 1/5 belong to fresh water.

Within the boundaries of Georgia Black sea never freezes that is not the case in its Northern part. Thanks to this the port cities of Georgia are available and operate the whole year.

In the coastline of Black sea recreational season lasts several months. There are numerous resorts (Batumi, Kobuleti, Kindgi, Gagra, etc.) and beach of international standards (Kvariati, Shekvetili, Ureki). Sea resorts are surrounded by mountains covered with rich vegetation that increases their esthetic and recreational importance.

99 LIMESTONE MASSIFS

Limestone massif of Askhi is located in Western Georgia, on the Egrisi mountain range, 40 km from the city of Kutaisi, between several historical and geographic provinces (Imereti, Lechkhumi and Samegrelo). Limestone massif is a part of a watershed of rivers Tekhuri and Tskhenistskali. Its highest peak is on 2529 meters above the sea level. The relative height of its upright slopes attains 1 km creating a very appealing scenery.

Limestone massif of Askhi is one of the most stretched and high in the boundaries of a limestone strip of Kavkasioni. Its area is more than 400 sq. km. The upper part of the massif is flat resembling a table and represents various karst forms.

Within the limestone massif of Askhi there are more than eight karst hollows with 42 caves among them. The total length of karst hollows is 4 km and its area exceeds 24 thousand sq. m. In the underground there are numerous brooks, rivers and lakes. Some of caves are natural glaciers as here ice is preserved nearly the whole year. Thera are also live organisms the most dispersed among them being Limonia fly (Limonia nubeculoza).

In some karst caves of Limestone massif of Askhi were discovered settlements of Stone Age humanoids, various tools and remnants of ancient animals (aurochs, cave bear, cave lynx). In Middle Ages both natural and man-made caves had the function of a shelter and a fortified facility.

Limestone massif of Khvamli is located in Western Georgia, in the southern part of Lechkhumi mountain range, on the watershed of rivers Rioni and Tskhenistskali, 25 km from the city of Kutaisi. Its area (83 sq.km) is relatively negligible, however comparable height attains a kilometer.

Limestone massif of Khvamli looks like a pyramid southern and western knees of which are steeper than northern and eastern ones. Western slopes are nearly vertical, their upper part is 300 meters high. Caves represented here were considered to be in one of the least accessible places in Georgia, therefore Georgian kings from XIII century used these caves for safe-keeping of treasures. As the legend goes, near the Limestone massif of Khvamli, in the gorge of river Tskaltsitela, lies Jason cave where ancient settlement of human beings was discovered.

In spite of a small area, there are many karst formations. Their number is 20 and total length attains 1 kilometer. Among them it is worth noting a fortified cave of Khvamli, Boga cave and Tekenteri well. Fortified cave on Plate is a historical monument. Its area is 60 sq.m. In the spacious Boga cave are represented ice stalactites and stalagmites used by the population for treatment purposes. In Tekenteri well with the depth of 16 meters it is only possible to descent from beech-tree hollow. It is also known that Khvamli massif caves are connected with each other via 'corridors'.

From Khvamli massif opens a magnificent panorama. From this point within one's sight are Central Kavkasioni and its summits, Kolkheti lowland and Ajara-Imereti range, towns and villages of inter-mountain valley.

1. Askhi
2. Khvamli

100 GEOMORPHOLOGICAL ROCKS

There are hundreds of enormous geomorphological remnant rocks in Georgia from which several stand out with their scale, one-of-a-kind nature and importance.

Pole of Katskhi is located in Western Georgia, on the urban territory of the town of Chiatura. It rises above the surface of the ground for 40 meters. It has the form of a right angle with the sides of 17 and 10 meters. The slopes of the Pole descend vertically and because of that climbing the Pole is possible only with special equipment. The environs of the Pole of Katskhi and its top are dressed in deciduous plants and lianas creating an inimitable landscape. In early and Middle ages the top of the Pole of Katskhi used to be a hide-out and a place of worship for anchorites. Two small churches were built on the surface of it.

Kvatsantsala is a limestone boulder situated in Western Georgia, Tsalenjikha region, 1800 meters above the sea level. Its weight is more that 10 tons, however it is enough just to push it lightly with a hand to start it moving.

The Pole of Bodorni is situated to the north of Tbilisi, in Dusheti region, on the right bank of river Aragvi, on the range of Eastern exposition of Alevi slope, 813 m above the sea level. It was generated in neogenic conglomerates, in the naturally cemented cobblestone environment. The height of the Pole is 15 meters and diameter of the basis – 4 meters. Within the frame of the Pole of Bodorni there are several

artificial caves which had been used in the past for worship and fortifying purposes. The Pole of Bodorni was awarded the status of a 'natural memorial'.

Kvabtatana is a granite eratic boulder situated in Western Georgia, in the basin of upper flow of river Rioni, 1357 meters above the sea level. Boulder is the 'witness' of the outreach of the last icing period with the help of which it is possible to ascertain the lower boundaries of the extent of Kavkasioni glaciers.

1. Katskhi
2. Pole of Bodorni
3. Kvatsantsala

GEORGIAN GRAPES

Georgia is considered to be the source of cultivated grapevines. Archeological excavations discovered ancient satsnakheli (grapes pressing tub), kvevri (clay vats for keeping wine), different tools and utencils used in viticulture. On the territory of Kvemo Kartli during archeological excavations were found grapes seeds of VI-V millenium. The culture of vine played a leading role in both heathen and Christian era in Georgia. Dispersion of Christian religion in Georgia is widely linked to the culture of vine. Saint Nino entered Georgia and preached Christianity with the Cross of Vine. Georgian churches are often adorned with images of grapes. Georgian churches and monasteries had primitive wine-manufacturing facilities, even today one can see marani (wine cellar) and satsnakheli there. Tradition of making wine in monasteries continues today.

Part of the Georgian household (living) estate is marani made of wood, stone or brick. Marani consists of satsnakheli and kvevri (clay vats). In Eastern Georgia marani is situated indoors (often in a basement), in Western Georgia it is usually outdoors, in a courtyard. All kinds of activities connected with brewing and keeping wine take place in marani. Often marani is the venue of a table party, therefore paraphernalia needed for arranging a feast is available in marani as well.

In Georgia grapes harvest is called rtveli. Rtveli starts in eastern Georgia at the end of September and continues two weeks. In western Georgia rtveli starts one month later.

There are up to 500 varieties of grapes in Georgia 1/10 of which are processed in the wine industry. Widely dispersed are such varieties as Rkatsiteli, Saperavi, Tsolikauri, Mtsvane, Tsitska, Ojaleshi, Chkhaveri, Alexandrouli, Aladasturi, Khikhvi, Krakhuna and others. Well known are also imported varietires (Aligote, Pinot, Chardonnay, Cabernet and others) which are well fitted with natural environment.

Dispersion of grapes in Georgia stretches over 900-1000 meters above the sea level, but the best natural (climate) conditions for it exist in the space of up to 700 meters above the sea level. In the relatively high uplands grow early harvest varieties of grapes, and in the lowlands - long and medium hang time varieties.

We meet grapes in every region of Georgia, however distinguished with its culture are Kakheti and Imereti, Kartli and Racha-Lechkhumi. World famous Georgian wine is on sale nowadays in up to fifty countries.

1. Marani in Eastern Georgia
2. Satsnakheli of Middle ages (Ikalto monastery, Kakheti)
3. Wooden satsnakheli and marani utencils (Western Georgia)

118

GEORGIAN DWELLING

Georgian dwelling (a house, a courtyard and a plot of land) fits in with geographic environment of Georgia. Back in history, in the different corners of Georgia, emerged a landscape-friendly living space. In the mountainous Georgia (Svaneti, Tusheti, Khevsureti) several-floor tower-houses built with cobblestone were popular to tackle severe climate and outer threat. In the plain of eastern Georgia (Kartli-Kakheti) a hall-type house built of cobblestone was popular because of hot summer and cold winter. In western Georgia (Imereti, Guria, Samegrelo, Racha-Lechkhumi, Abkhazia) due to mild climate we come across wooden built, wide-terrace oda-houses or fern-knitted patskha (hut). In Southern Georgia except Shavshuri oda houses (popular in Ajara and Samtskhe) there are houses with earth roofs (in Javakheti with severe climate).

In 1966 a noted Georgian ethnographer, Giorgi Chitaya has established Ethnographic Museum under the Sky in western part of Tbilisi, near Turtle lake. There are specimens of houses and other support buildings (grain stockroom, maize stockroom, marani...) represented here.

Important segment of the Georgian traditional estate is Georgian marani. Marani is not only a place where wine is brought and stocked. It is traditionally a sacrosanct place for a family, where consecrated Eucharist wine is kept. Invitation of a guest to marani meant bestowing special honors to him/her. In eastern Georgia marani is closed and is used for basement purposes. In Western Georgia marani is usually placed

on the lifted point and kvevri, or vats are buried in the ground without a shelter. Among many paraphernalia of marani satsnakheli (grapes-pressing tub), a corner for distilling vodka (it is called zaot in Kakheti) and others should be mentioned. Diverse utencils and items used in wine industry are also kept in marani.

Exibits of Ethnographic Museum under the Sky:
1. Kartli-type House from Tskhinvali region
2. Imeretian Oda-House
3. Megrelian Oda
4. Manor of Kakheti Prince (XIX c.)
5. Hall-type House (Shida Kartli)

CONTENTS